CW01270108

Seduced by a Sociopath

Seduced BY A SOCIOPATH

How antisocials, narcissists and psychopaths use human nature against you

DONNA ANDERSEN

Anderly Publishing
Egg Harbor Township, New Jersey

© 2019 by Donna Andersen

All rights reserved. No part of this publication may be reproduced, stored in a retrieval system, or transmitted in any form or by any means, electronic, mechanical, photocopying, recording, or otherwise—other than for "fair use" as brief quotations embodied in articles and reviews—without the written permission of the publisher.

Back cover photography by Bill Horin

Anderly Publishing
3121-D Fire Road, #304
Egg Harbor Township, NJ 08234 USA
www.anderlypublishing.com

Library of Congress Control Number: 2019954557
ISBN: 978-1-951347-03-1

First softcover edition November 2019

Contents

Introduction 15

10 red flags of a sociopath that I saw but did not understand......18

Why relationships with sociopaths are so addictive 23

If you feel an emotional void, the sociopath will step in...........27

12 seduction strategies from the sociopath playbook................31

8 ways your body warns you about sociopaths 34

29 excuses that sabotage our instincts about sociopaths..........37

Oxytocin, trust and why we fall for psychopaths 40

9 control tactics in a classic story of sociopathic manipulation 45

The psychopath and our own self-image 49

10 terms to help you name your experience with a sociopath......52

How to protect yourself from sociopaths in 3 easy steps..........56

13 very early warning signs that your new partner may be a controller 60

Sociopaths target our dreams 64

7 fake reasons why sociopaths seem so romantic 69

Love, sex, your brain and sociopaths 73

8 reasons why we can't see what's wrong with the sociopath 77

How sociopaths intentionally mess with your mind 79

7 reasons not to have sex with a sociopath 82

Sociopaths and their multiple simultaneous manipulation strategies 85

10 signs you're addicted to loving a cheater 88

Are these warning signs that I'm involved with a sociopath? 91

Sociopaths say you're crazy – and you believe them 93

11 abusive behaviors you're likely to see from a sociopathic partner 97

6 really bad reasons for staying with the sociopath 101

4 reasons why psychopaths will never stop cheating 104

Why falling for a romance scam doesn't mean you're stupid 107

Deception: the sociopath's key strategy 111

Why did I want to hug the sociopath, even though I know he is bad? 113

5 reasons why we fall for con artists 118

Seriously lacking: 'Savvy Senior' advice about online dating......121

To the psychopath, the relationship meant nothing 125

To Mom and Dad: 9 reasons why your son or daughter fell for the sociopath 127

Psychopathy can run in families —a possible warning for you132

3 steps to prevent a sociopath from taking advantage of your vulnerabilities...136

Why we fall for romance scams 139

5 reasons why you can hook up with multiple sociopaths 145

Will emotional abuse become physical abuse? 149

Sociopaths use our self-image against us 153

Getting over that amazing 'chemistry' 157

A sociopath claims, 'We are evolution's next step' 163

What if you see some signs of a sociopath, but not all of them?..165

Are sociopaths opportunists? 171

The sociopath's isolation campaign: Keeping you from the people you love 173

Sociopaths use our own dreams to seduce us.........................176

9 questions to help you discern if your caring, helpful partner is faking it 180

10 reasons why the fireworks of a romance with a sociopath are duds 183

Letter to Lovefraud: He flat out admits he is a sociopath 185

Emotional and psychological abuse, described by 12 Lovefraud readers 192

Letter to Lovefraud: Should I warn the next victim? 195

Here's the absolutely best way to protect yourself from sociopaths 199

How knowing the truth about sociopaths changes everything 201

About the author 204

Introduction

"You sound delightful!" Those were the first words James Alwyn Montgomery wrote to me after I responded to his online dating ad back in 1996.

I didn't know it at the time, but James Montgomery, my future husband, had just commenced his love bombing campaign. Multiple times a day, he called, emailed and faxed (this was before text). He brought me little gifts every time we got together. Our relationship quickly became physical, and he wanted us to mark on our calendars, in advance, which nights we would spend together, and whether we'd be at his home, or mine.

I was swept off my feet in a whirlwind romance.

I didn't know that this was a warning sign of sociopathic seduction.

Nobody did. No one was talking about sociopaths, narcissists or psychopaths in 1996. In fact, when I launched Lovefraud.com in 2005, it was one of the first websites on the Internet to expose romance scams.

My original intention with Lovefraud was to warn people about con artists who target romantic partners in order to take their money. But as readers began telling me their stories, I learned that these thieves of hearts aren't always looking for financial gain. Sometimes they're looking for a place to live. Sometimes they're looking for someone to provide services, such as cooking, cleaning and childcare. Sometimes they want a partner who can enhance their image in the community. And sometimes they look for hearts to break, just for the fun of it.

How, exactly, do they do it? How do they convince unsuspecting men and women, like me and you, to trust them, fall in love with them, and give them everything they want?

Lovefraud has the answers. I've written many articles explaining what sociopaths do, how they do it and why the rest of us respond to them. With this book, the articles on sociopathic seduction are collected in one place.

You'll learn the tactics that sociopaths employ, and how normal people are affected, psychologically and even biologically. You'll learn why we fall for the seduction, and why, even when we realize we're in a bad situation, it's so difficult to escape.

If this you've had this experience, you'll feel validated. You certainly are not alone.

What, exactly, is a sociopath?

Long after I divorced him, James Montgomery was professionally diagnosed as a psychopath. Psychopathy is similar to, but not precisely the same as, antisocial personality disorder. Both psychopaths and antisocials engage in narcissistic behavior, but mental health professionals also recognize a separate diagnosis of narcissistic personality disorder. People with these disorders routinely manipulate others, as do those with borderline and histrionic personality disorders.

In other words, identifying these human predators is a mess. There are multiple clinical diagnoses for people who exploit and manipulate others. To simplify matters, on Lovefraud.com, I use the word "sociopathy" as an umbrella term to cover all of these disorders. Although today many professionals use "sociopathy" as a synonym for antisocial personality disorder, its original meaning was broader.

When psychologist George E. Partridge coined the term "sociopathy" in 1930, he wanted it to mean, "anything deviated or pathological in social relations." In his view, the word described a pathological condition in which people are maladjusted in their relations with others and society, and motivated towards antisocial behavior. This perfectly describes anyone who has an-

Introduction

tisocial, narcissistic, borderline, histrionic or psychopathic personality disorders.

For you, the precise diagnosis probably doesn't matter. You just need to be able to spot these destructive individuals and get them out of your life.

Best of the Lovefraud Blog Series

Lovefraud.com now has more than 4,000 articles spread out over years of blog archives. It's great stuff, but particular articles are not always easy to find. To make the information more accessible, I've collected and organized the articles into specific themes for this *Best of the Lovefraud Blog* series of books:

- *Understanding the Sociopath*
- *Seduced by a Sociopath*
- *Dealing with Sociopaths*
- *Recovery from a Sociopath*

The articles in this collection were written over many years, so in some cases I have updated them.

If you now realize, to your shock and dismay, that you are, or have been, in a romantic relationship with a sociopath, *Seduced by a Sociopath* explains how it happened. Understanding how you were targeted, and why you responded, is the first step towards your escape and recovery.

10 red flags of a sociopath that I saw but did not understand

Yes, the red flags were there. Like you, I saw behaviors in the man I married (far too quickly) that were warning signs of his sociopathic personality disorder. Like you, I didn't know what they meant.

My book, *Red Flags of Love Fraud — 10 signs you're dating a sociopath,* reveals the tactics of social predators who pursue romantic relationships not for love, but for exploitation. This book explains how sociopaths seduce their targets, why it's hard to escape the relationships, and how you can protect yourself.

Most people targeted by sociopaths actually see the warning signs, but don't know how to interpret them. *Red Flags of Love Fraud* explains the patterns of behavior, so you can tell the difference between real love and exploitation.

I, of course, was the original guinea pig for the book. I met my ex-husband, James Montgomery, on the Internet more than 20 years ago. He was a widower, originally from Australia, but at the time living near me in New Jersey. He told me he was a Hollywood screenwriter, successful entrepreneur and military hero. He was none of those, but unfortunately, at the time, I didn't know to be on the lookout for lies.

So here are some of the Red Flags of Love Fraud that I missed with Montgomery.

1. Charisma and charm

Montgomery had a magnetic energy about him. He was smooth,

confident, always knew what to say, never missed a beat. He was prolific in admiration and praise for me — especially in the beginning.

Initially, every time we got together, he had a gift for me. Even then, I suspected that the gifts had belonged to his recently deceased wife, but I let it slide — I was pleased that he was thinking of me. I later learned that he had a habit of stealing from one woman he was involved with to give gifts to another.

2. Sudden soul mates

Montgomery told me that I was the woman he'd been waiting for all his life. We were both writers. We were both entrepreneurs. We had so much in common, that it must be fate — we were destined to be together!

He also told me that because we were so right for each other, he'd never feel the need to cheat again. That statement should have been a double red flag with sirens blaring. But I accepted it at face value — with me, unlike with my predecessors, Montgomery would be faithful.

In reality, he cheated with multiple women throughout our relationship.

3. Sexual magnetism

Yes, there was sex. In the beginning, there was lots of sex, and it was rambunctious. I interpreted the sex as an indication of Montgomery's desire for me. In fact, when he sent me an erotic short story, starring James and Donna, I was flattered — no man had ever written a sexy story for me.

Except, he didn't write the story. He stole it from one of his previous women. After that, he sent it out to all his women — just insert the latest target's name. When he forgot to change all the names, he received an angry email from one of his other targets demanding to know, "Who is this Donna chick?"

4. Love bombing

From the moment I responded to James Montgomery's dating profile, he poured it on. Phone calls, emails, faxes (this was before social media). He proclaimed his love, sent me poetry, flattered me by asking for my opinion on his business issues.

Then he claimed to be going on a clandestine overseas mission, but he was so smitten that he moved heaven and earth to come back and visit me in the middle of it. Afterwards, of course, I learned that he never left the county — he was entertaining another woman in his deceased wife's townhome.

5. Blames others for everything

Why did his grandiose plans to build a new type of entertainment venue fall through? The government took his land! (He never had the land to begin with.)

Why was his credit card declined? Investors were trying to squeeze him for a better deal! (There were no investors.)

Eventually it became, why didn't we have any money? Because I didn't have faith in him! It was all my fault!

6. Lies and gaps in the story

I will admit, the lies that I caught early on were so minor that they were easy to overlook. Like, if Montgomery and his wife had just come to New Jersey in the past year, how did she go to a particular shoe store two years earlier?

To cover his big lies — like his fake military service — Montgomery was totally consistent in his story, saying the same thing to everyone. He fabricated documentation to back up his claims. But what was really convincing was the sheer brazenness of his statements. Who would lie about earning Australia's highest military honor during the Vietnam War? I didn't know that a sociopath would.

7. Intense eye contact

Anyone who believes liars can't look you in the eye — well, they haven't been lied to by a sociopath. I remember all the times Montgomery looked into my eyes and made statements and promises that I now know to be total lies.

Sometimes, the eyes of a sociopath appear to be empty or dead, and that's what I saw more of. At times, Montgomery appeared to be staring blankly, as if nobody was home inside. And that was exactly the case.

8. Moves fast to hook up

Within a few days of us meeting in person, Montgomery wanted us to coordinate our schedules, planning in advance when we would spend the night at his house, and when we would stay at my house.

Then he wanted us to marry before the end of the year, supposedly so that I would be eligible to receive benefits from his military pension. Of course, he was never in the military, so the whole story was a ruse to get his hooks into me faster.

9. Pity play

Montgomery plotted our entire initial meeting around the pity play. First he pulled out his wedding pictures with his previous wife who died, to make me feel bad for the poor, grieving widower.

Then when I expressed hesitation — it might be too soon for him to become involved with a new relationship — his eyes became moist. He talked about all the people he'd lost — his wife, his father, his buddies from Vietnam — and how he needed to move on. (He did lose his father and wife, but there were no buddies from Vietnam.)

10. Jekyll and Hyde personality

Montgomery wanted me to convert my basement into an office for him, which I agreed to do (and paid for). It wasn't fancy, but he was happy. Then, when he was angry at me, he complained about being forced to work in a cellar. Then he was happy again, and the basement was fine. Then he hated it again.

So did Montgomery like his office? Or did he hate it? I have no idea. But his changing whims served their purpose — they kept me off balance.

Relationships from hell

Red Flags of Love Fraud is about the real relationships from hell. They usually start out as a whirlwind of love and romance, and then, sooner or later, spiral down into lies, cheating, manipulation and abuse. They are the worst relationships you can imagine, but they are totally preventable if you know how to read the warning signs.

Why relationships with sociopaths are so addictive

Time and time again, when I do personal consultations, people tell me how they struggle to break away from a relationship with a sociopath.

You know the involvement is bad for you. But even when you're not forced to interact with the sociopath — you're not married, don't have kids with the person and don't work together — you can't cut the cord.

Why? Because relationships with sociopaths are highly addictive.

There are psychological and biological reasons for this, which I'll explain.

Psychological bond

Any time two human beings enter into a relationship, a psychological love bond forms.

This bond begins early in the relationship because of pleasure. In the beginning, both people are doing their best to attract and impress each other. The new involvement is fun and exciting, which creates the pleasure.

Sociopaths, of course, usually engage in love bombing. They shower you with attention and affection. They're always calling and texting. They want to be with you all the time. The sociopath makes you feel like the most important and loved person in the world. This intensifies your pleasure.

The relationship seems to be moving ahead at warp speed, and then the sociopath does something to threaten the relationship — disappears, lies, picks a fight. You were once on cloud nine, and now you suddenly feel totally deflated. This creates fear and anxiety.

Now here's the kicker: Fear and anxiety actually strengthen the psychological love bond.

You want the relationship to go back to how wonderful it was in the beginning. So you ask the sociopath if you can talk. You try to figure out what went wrong. You may even apologize for something you didn't do.

You get back together with the sociopath, which brings you relief — and strengthens the psychological love bond again.

This becomes a pattern: Pleasure, followed by fear and anxiety, followed by relief, rinse and repeat. It becomes a vicious circle, and with each turn of the wheel, the psychological love bond gets tighter and tighter.

Here's the next kicker: Even if you no longer feel pleasure, the psychological bond is still in place.

Pleasure is required for the bond to form. But the absence of pleasure does not break the bond.

Biological bond

There are also biological reasons why you feel so attached to the sociopath.

When you experience intimacy, the neurotransmitter oxytocin is released in your brain and bloodstream. This happens with any type of intimacy — emotional sharing, hugs and especially sex.

Oxytocin is called the "cuddle chemical." It makes you feel calm, trusting and content, and alleviates fear and anxiety. Mother Nature created oxytocin to make parents want to stay together to raise children. It is critical for the survival of the human race.

But, oxytocin also makes you want to stay with someone when you really should leave.

Feelings of love also make the brain produce dopamine. Dopamine is associated with energy, motivation and addiction. In fact, that's why cocaine makes people feel euphoric — it increases the amount of dopamine in the brain.

There's more. Sex also causes structural changes in the brain. So if you have sex with a sociopath, your brain changes to adapt to this person. Breaking off the relationship will require undoing all the changes in your brain.

Sociopaths don't bond

Human beings are social animals, and we need to be able to trust each other and stay together to survive. That's why these psychological and biological changes take place.

However, sociopaths don't bond like regular, empathic people do. Some researchers theorize that sociopathic brains don't have the right receptors for oxytocin.

But they have learned how to pretend to be in a relationship, in order to set you up for exploitation. Sociopaths hijack the normal human bonding process.

Breaking the addiction

Because of these psychological and biological reasons, relationships with sociopaths are highly addictive. So when you want to break away from a sociopath, you need to treat it like breaking an addiction.

Here's what this means.

First: In most cases, you'll want to go cold turkey when breaking off the relationship. That means you tell sociopath very clearly that it's over. Here's what I recommend that you say, which is adapted from *The Gift of Fear* by Gavin de Becker:

I have no romantic interest in you whatsoever.
I am certain I never will.
Do not contact me ever again.

Do not give a reason for breaking up, because a reason gives a sociopath an opportunity to argue with you. You do not want to attempt to negotiate with a sociopath, because the sociopath will usually win.

Second: Once you make it clear that the involvement is over, have No Contact with the sociopath. You'll find more information about how to implement no contact on Lovefraud.com

Third: If you've ever had to overcome addiction — smoking, alcohol, drugs — you probably know that the standard advice is to take it one day at a time. That's exactly what you need to do when detoxing from a sociopath.

Get through today. Then get through tomorrow. Then get through the next day. Do whatever you need to do to distract yourself from any urges to contact the person. The longer you stay away from the sociopath, the more his or her grip on you will dissipate.

If you give in and reach out to the sociopath, or answer when the sociopath contacts you, you'll be back at square one. You'll have to start the process all over again.

Fourth: When you're feeling the urge to contact the sociopath, visit Lovefraud. Many, many people have told me that they do this. They read the posts and comments on Lovefraud to remind them of why they are leaving.

Like overcoming any addiction, disengaging from a sociopath takes time and willpower. But your emotions, mind, body, spirit and finances will all be healthier away from this person.

If you feel an emotional void, the sociopath will step in

I recently received email from a woman whom we'll call "Adriana:"

> I am told I am a very beautiful, intelligent, fun, woman, but that is all subjective. I am 61 years old but pass for late 40's; good genes. I have been divorced for 10 years and engaged once during that time. I have dated so many men and feel that I have no purpose because I can't find "him." I don't find most men attractive — don't have chemistry with them and I don't want to settle. I have not been successful in love at all and have tried to look within myself to see my faults, but the truth is I just want to love and be loved.
>
> Anyway, I am so tired of dating and getting my hopes up each time I meet someone I really am attracted to. I was setting up a booth for a trade show and a man from the booth a few down came by and gave me a bottle of water (he is a manager for a water company) and I said thanks and did not really pay much attention to him — he was ok looking.
>
> The next day he was all dressed up looked so nice and he came to my booth looked me dead in the eyes and said "so where are you taking me to lunch?" I was so charmed by his approach and of course we ended up having lunch and then went out that night, but he conned me into dinner then back to his apt. Where he put the move on me.

I am a savvy woman, but I must have been stupid. We spent the weekend together and he began to change plans on me, would get all emotional and cry but I never saw any tears, anyway bottom line is he is a liar, he never asked me for money ever, but the rest of the stuff on your sociopath list he is guilty of.

Everything is about HIM AND ONLY HIM, I think his cold/hot actions were to throw me off and keep me under his control. Anyway my question is, how could I have such deep feelings for this man I have known for two weeks, and if he is only like eight out of your 10 markers, does that mean he is not a sociopath? He has done so much damage to me that I prayed to die. I feel worthless, unworthy, lonely, and I still miss the jerk.

I tried to level with him and told him no more games, I wanted to be loved and he said he could not give me that now. That was the first honest thing he said to me I think.

Please help me figure out if he is or is not a sociopath.

Adriana's first question was, "How can I have such deep feelings for this man I have known for two weeks?" The answer: Adriana was the target of calculated seduction.

She didn't provide a lot of detail about her interaction. But a man who walks up and says, "Where are you taking me to lunch?" has obviously targeted her. So I assume he also employed the rest of the strategies in the sociopath's playbook, such as love bombing and the sudden soul mates tactics. I explain them all in my book, *Red Flags of Love Fraud—10 signs you're dating a sociopath*. The bottom line is that for two weeks, Adriana was probably subjected to over-the-top attention, and she responded.

About her second question—If Adriana saw eight out of the 10 Red Flags of Love Fraud, then that's warning enough. It doesn't matter if the guy doesn't completely qualify as a sociopath, he certainly qualifies as bad news, and that's exactly what I told her.

Emotional void

But reading this email, I was more concerned about Adriana's

If you feel an emotional void the sociopath will step in

frame of mind. She came out and said, "I feel that I have no purpose because I can't find 'him.'"

This is precisely the type of emotional void that a sociopath will happily step into.

I am not criticizing Adriana. I know exactly how she feels, because I once felt the same way. I was smart, successful, attractive, looked younger than my years—and none of that made any difference to me because I was without a partner.

The emptiness in my heart was certainly palpable to me—and perhaps to the sociopath as well. James Montgomery quickly figured out that I was an easy target. He complimented me, poured on the attention, proclaimed I was the woman he'd been waiting for all his life, painted a shimmering picture of how wonderful our life together would be—and I swallowed it all, hook, line and sinker.

Vulnerabilities

Sociopaths specialize in preying on lonely people. So if you are walking around with a big hole in your heart instead of the fulfillment of love, imagine that you are also walking around with a big, red target tattooed on your forehead. KNOW THAT YOU ARE VULNERABLE.

Sociopaths have an uncanny ability to sense emptiness. For this reason, if you feel lonely, it is critically important that you know the Red Flags of Love Fraud. Because sociopaths all seem to use exactly the same strategies and tactics, I'm beginning to believe that involvements with these destructive individuals are totally preventable, if you know what to look for, and, if you spot the signs, you get out.

But you also need to know yourself. Sociopaths target vulnerabilities, and there are many more vulnerabilities besides loneliness. You can be overly trusting. You can be wounded from past betrayals. You can be suffering from grief.

Vulnerabilities are not necessarily flaws. We are all vulnerable in some way. It's part of being human. In fact, we must allow ourselves to be vulnerable in order to have a fulfilling relationship. But we must recognize that vulnerabilities also leave us open to exploitation by sociopaths.

Red Flags of Love Fraud Workbook

To help you become aware of your vulnerabilities, and recognize when someone is trying to take advantage of you, I've put together a companion for my new book called the *Red Flags of Love Fraud Workbook.*

It's a small book—only 40 pages—with checklists and questions to ask yourself, and spaces to record your answers. Its purpose is to enable you to think carefully about your internal reality, so you can strengthen your resistance to predators. And if you've already been snagged by a sociopath, answering the questions will help you figure out how it happened, and what you have to do to get out of the involvement.

The workbook is available in the Lovefraud Store.

The key to keeping sociopaths out of your life is to know that they exist, know the warning signs, and know yourself. The two *Red Flags of Love Fraud* books give you the tools you need to stay safe and healthy.

12 seduction strategies from the sociopath playbook

Sociopaths tend to use all the same tactics while reeling in new romantic partners, as if they were all working from the same well-known reference manual. If you were able to find this playbook, written by an alpha sociopath for the benefit of the trainees, here are ploys it would include:

1. Listen intently to your targets, staring into their eyes and hanging on their every word

This encourages them to keep talking — and everything they tell you can later be used as ammunition against them.

2. Call, text and email your targets frequently

They will interpret your constant attention as a sign that you are smitten with them, and will not notice that you are establishing control over them.

3. Mirror your targets

What your targets really want is to see their own images reflected in your eyes. Convince them that you like everything they like and share all their values, and they will believe that the two of you are soul mates.

4. Proclaim your love quickly and loudly

Because most normal people hesitate to talk about their feelings, your targets will assume that you are head-over-heels in love with them, so much so that you must express your emotions. This will smash their defenses.

5. If your targets at first rebuff your advances, pursue, pursue, pursue

When you keep at it, the targets will eventually believe that you are genuinely interested in them, and wanting to be fair and nonjudgmental, they will believe that they should give you a chance. This will be the opening that you can exploit.

6. Create a whirlwind romance

When you keep your targets spinning, they lose their balance and become easier to manipulate.

7. Give your targets gifts, no matter how small

This will make your targets feel the need to reciprocate, which will increase their investment in the relationship.

8. Make your targets feel sorry for you

The juiciest targets are empathetic people, and empaths must respond to pitiful stories. Their empathy will keep them hooked.

9. Bed your targets as quickly as possible

Sex floods your targets with oxytocin, a neurotransmitter and hormone that is called nature's love glue. Oxytocin makes your targets trust you. The more sex, the more they trust you, and the more you can manipulate them. Plus, you'll probably enjoy the sex.

10. Find your targets' vulnerabilities

Discover their deepest needs, fears and desires. When you set your hook firmly into their most private vulnerabilities, they will not be able to escape.

11. To win your target back, employ the grand gesture

If you do something that hurts or angers your target — hey,

nobody's perfect — you may need extraordinary measures to get back on track. Perhaps an extravagant gift (steal it if you have to), or an extraordinary date (figure out a way to get them to pay for it), or get on your knee in front of their friends and family to propose. They'll succumb, and will be more bonded to you than ever.

12. Ask about your targets' hopes and dreams, and promise to make them come true

This has the effect of making it very difficult for the targets to leave, because if they give up on the relationship, they also must give up on their hopes and dreams.

It's scary to think that there might be such a reference manual floating around, teaching disordered people these strategies to seduce their targets.

The truth is even more frightening — sociopaths just do what comes naturally.

8 ways your body warns you about sociopaths

It took millions of years for our species to evolve from apes to modern humans, and during those years we spent a lot of time fleeing for our lives. Our very survival depended upon being able to sense danger from predators. We still have the ability to sense danger, although today it comes not from saber-toothed tigers, but from human predators, aka sociopaths.

This protective sense is our intuition, which is part instinctive knowing, and part physical reaction. Our bodies tell us when someone or a situation poses a threat. Here are eight ways that our bodies warn us of danger:

1. **Fear.** This is the ultimate warning sign. If you are ever suddenly gripped by fear when someone is in your presence, consider it the strongest possible warning.
2. **Chills.** If someone looks at you like you're the next meal, and the hair on the back of your neck stands up, you could be reacting to a sociopath's predatory stare.
3. **Difficulty breathing.** When you find it hard to take deep, even breaths around the person, it's probably because something about their behavior is profoundly troublesome.

4. **Crying.** When your interactions with this person frequently bring you to tears, know that this is not normal. It's a warning that something is terribly amiss.
5. **Pounding heart.** This may not be excitement or attraction. It may signify that deep down, you're afraid.
6. **Upset stomach.** If you feel nauseous around a person, or when you think about certain interactions that you've had with the person, perhaps your internal compass is sending you a message.
7. **Nightmares**. If you have bad dreams while involved with a person, or you have difficulty sleeping, pay attention. Something is interfering with your rest.
8. **Nagging feeling.** You have a sense that something is wrong, but you can't identify what it is. Your inner self knows there is a problem, and is trying to get your attention.

Pay attention to physical warning signs

The key to escaping sociopaths is to pay attention when you experience warning signs like these. Unfortunately, we often don't listen to ourselves.

One Lovefraud reader told me that a stranger walked into her office, and she was immediately terrified. Instead of recognizing the internal warning, the woman berated herself for being paranoid. So rather than avoid the man, she accepted his overtures and started dating him. Well, he was a sociopath, and the relationship turned out to be a complete nightmare.

Most people experience warning signs early in an involvement, but don't know what they mean. In the Lovefraud Romantic Partner Survey, I asked a question about this. I asked, "Did you have an intuition or gut instinct early in the involvement that there was something wrong with the person or the relationship?" An astounding 71 percent of survey respondents answered yes. But 40 percent of respondents ignored their intuition and continued with the relationship — much to their later regret.

So if you instinctively have a bad reaction to someone, don't chide yourself for being judgmental or paranoid. Don't tell yourself that everyone deserves a chance and you should be open-minded. There is a reason for your reaction, even if you don't know what it is right away.

If you can't avoid the person altogether, at least be wary. Your intuition is probably trying to warn you of danger.

29 excuses that sabotage our instincts about sociopaths

Almost all of us have an instinctive warning that something is terribly wrong early in an involvement with a sociopath (antisocial, narcissist, borderline, histrionic, psychopath). Almost all of us ignore the warning.

Last week I wrote about the physical symptoms that we often feel in *8 ways your body warns you about sociopaths*. I included fear, chills, difficulty breathing, crying, pounding heart, upset stomach, nightmares and a nagging feeling. The post was widely shared, and several Lovefraud readers added more physical warning signs: immobilizing exhaustion, poor appetite, nervous tension, tiredness, cloudy thinking, vague upset, tightness in the chest.

When we're involved with a predator, our bodies desperately try to get our attention to warn us of the danger. Unfortunately, our minds override our instincts, even when the disordered individual is engaging in damaging or hurtful behavior.

Our partner does something mean or selfish. Or our partner acts coldly towards us. Or we catch the individual in a lie, or suspect that he/she is cheating. But instead of recognizing the behavior as a potential deal-breaker, we explain it away.

Suppressing our instincts

Here are some of the stories and excuses that we tell ourselves to let our callous partners off the hook:

1. I must have misunderstood.
2. We all have our issues.
3. He/she really does love me.
4. I'm sure he/she didn't mean it.
5. He/she has been through so much (not knowing the stories are lies).
6. It must be true — no one would lie about something like that.
7. Everyone deserves a second chance.
8. I don't have any proof that he/she really did it (when suspecting bad behavior).
9. I'm going to give the unconditional love he/she has never had.
10. I've been hurt before and I'm just afraid that I'll be hurt again.
11. I'll prove that I'm different (after stories about the individual's exes).
12. He/she would never intentionally hurt me.
13. We just got our wires crossed.
14. I want to make my own decision (after warnings from other people).
15. I don't want to be judgmental.
16. He/she is stressed out.
17. I'm being paranoid.
18. If I bring up my concerns I'll upset him/her.
19. When I asked why it happened he/she had a plausible explanation.
20. I should always give the benefit of the doubt.
21. There's good in everyone.
22. He/she is just having a bad day.
23. I feel scared, but there's no reason for it, so I must be overreacting.
24. He/she is being so sweet to me — I feel bad for doubting him/her.
25. The last time I brought up an issue he/she was so hurt that I ended up apologizing.
26. I will not abandon him/her like everyone else did.

29 excuses that sabotage our instincts about sociopaths

27. He/she is doing such important work (after stories of the individual working for the FBI, CIA, etc.).
28. I just need to soothe the wounded child inside him/her.
29. I cannot base my judgment on a mere gut feeling.

Act on your instincts

Actually, yes, you can base your judgment on your gut feelings. Your personal relationship is not a court of law, and you do not need proof beyond a reasonable doubt when deciding whether or not to keep going with a romantic partner. If you get any intuitive hits at all, pay close attention.

In fact, that's the best way to protect yourself. You should not only listen to your instincts, but you should act on them. When your body is telling you that something is dreadfully wrong, don't let the wishful thinking of your mind overrule it.

Oxytocin, trust and why we fall for psychopaths

Invariably, once we realize we've been conned by a psychopath, this person has lied to us from the very beginning, and we fell for all of it, we ask why? Why did we believe? Why did we trust?

The short answer is that we did what we, as social animals, are biologically designed to do. Human beings have evolved over millennia to live in community, and trust is the glue that holds us together.

I just finished reading *The Moral Molecule — the source of love and prosperity,* by Paul J. Zak. Zak spent 10 years researching a brain chemical called oxytocin and its role in human behavior. He says oxytocin inspires trust; trust is connected to morality; and morality is connected to the survival of the human race.

A video on Lovefraud gives an overview of the points he makes in his book. Zak briefly refers to psychopaths in the video, and the discussion about this personality disorder in his book isn't much longer. I'm going to extrapolate from his work to discuss the role that oxytocin probably plays in why psychopaths do what they do, and why we respond the way we do.

What is oxytocin?

Oxytocin is both a neurotransmitter, sending signals within the brain, and a hormone, carrying messages in the bloodstream. It plays a huge role in pair bonding, especially for monogamous mammals. It has long been associated with sex, childbirth and breastfeeding.

Research now shows that both men and women release oxytocin, although women release far more. The substance is integrally involved with love and empathy. An article in Scientific American describes oxytocin as Nature's "love glue."

Intimacy and sex trigger the release of oxytocin. So do feelings of empathy. An easy way to spark the release of oxytocin in people is to give them a hug. Another way is to show that you trust them. Conversation creates a sense of community, which builds trust, which leads to oxytocin release.

In his book, Zak describes a behavioral feedback loop based on oxytocin:

> Oxytocin generates the empathy that drives moral behavior, which inspires trust, which causes the release of more oxytocin, which creates more empathy.

But it's not all love and roses. Oxytocin also helps people know when to be wary. Zak says, "oxytocin maintains the balance between self and other, trust and distrust, approach and withdrawal."

Testosterone

Testosterone is a hormone associated with aggression, motivation and drive, especially sex drive. Men have more testosterone than women, and young men have twice the level of testosterone as older men. **Testosterone is elevated in all psychopaths, both male and female.** Hold that thought.

Testosterone is the opposite of oxytocin. In *The Moral Molecule,* Zak says:

> Testosterone *specifically* interferes with the uptake of oxytocin, producing a damping effect on being caring and feeling. (Page 83, emphasis by Zak.)

Zak also talks about a high-octane version of testosterone called dihydrotestosterone (DHT), which stimulates areas of the brain associated with aggression. Zak writes:

DHT's affect on the brain is about five times larger than testosterone's. It not only unleashes aggression, but also increases dopamine, which makes the aggression feel good. (Page 84)

Here are a few more points about testosterone:

High-testosterone males divorce more often, spend less time with their children, engage in competitions of all types, have more sexual partners (as well as learning disabilities), and lose their jobs more often. (Page 90)

Winning too big too often can have a corrosive effect by bathing an individual in testosterone. Always coming out on top, consistently and over time, can reinforce some of the more obnoxious stereotypically male behaviors associated with the hormone. (Page 94)

Administering testosterone has been shown to actually inhibit people's ability's to pick up the social cues that eye contact conveys. (Page 95)

Putting this together: Psychopaths have excess testosterone. Testosterone blocks caring and feeling, increases aggression, inhibits the ability to pick up on social cues and correlates with the type of behavior we've all seen in psychopaths.

Oxytocin receptors

Oxytocin works by connecting with "oxytocin receptors," which are present in the mammary glands, uterus and in the central nervous system. However, Zak says that "5 percent of any population lack the oxytocin receptors necessary to bond and behave morally without external reinforcement." Of course, 5 percent is remarkably close to official estimates for antisocial personality disorder — 4 percent of the population.

Zak explains that oxytocin receptors need to be stimulated, starting when humans are babies, in order for them to grow. If the receptors are not stimulated by love and attention early on, they fail to develop, which contributes to a lack of empathy. In an interview with IEEE Spectrum, Zak says that psychopaths seem to lack oxytocin receptors.

In *The Moral Molecule,* Zak writes:

> Psychopaths can have incredible social competence on the cognitive level — the trouble is that they simply don't care bout anyone but themselves. Their lack of empathy allows them to treat others as objects, and their cognitive skill enables them to get away with it. (Page 128)

Oxytocin and the psychopathic experience

Psychopaths do not form authentic, caring love bonds with other people. But they are very good at pretending that they do.

When psychopaths target us for romantic relationships, they shower us with attention and affection. They spend a lot of time talking with us, and conversation builds trust. They say and do things to indicate that they trust us, and we should trust them. They tell stories about themselves designed to appeal to our empathy. They rush us into emotional, physical and sexual intimacy.

All of this causes the release of oxytocin in our brains, which is absolutely normal. Because of the oxytocin, we feel calm, trusting, empathetic and content. We especially feel trusting of the person who caused this reaction in us — the psychopath.

The psychopath, however, does not have the normal number of oxytocin receptors. Plus, the psychopath has elevated testosterone, which blocks the release of oxytocin. Therefore, he or she does not experience the effects of the oxytocin, and does not feel trust or empathy.

Researchers are finding many biological components of psychopathy, including the problems with oxytocin. But the oxytocin system operates just fine in many of us who have been targeted by psychopaths. So they love bomb us; we don't know they are lying; we respond as human are intended to respond to displays of trust and affection, which releases oxytocin.

Psychopathic seduction hijacks the normal human bonding system. That's an important reason why we get hooked.

If you'd like to know more about oxytocin and how it is supposed to work, read *The Moral Molecule*, by Paul J. Zak.

9 control tactics in a classic story of sociopathic manipulation

The following letter, written by a young woman whom we'll call Chloe, is one of the most complete stories of psychological manipulation that I've seen yet. Chloe wrote this letter secretly while the sociopath she is living with was at the gym.

I met my boyfriend two years ago. I was 18; he was 33. He's a photographer; we live on an island that is very small. He has lived here forever (10 years) and I had only been here a few months when I met him. Everybody, especially women on the island, adore him, he is THE BIGGEST charmer.

He told me that he had moved here with his fiance, that she had said she was going home for a week, and then never came back. He said she'd gone to therapy back home and been "mindf*cked" and never returned, breaking their engagement. I felt for him. He was so normal and sweet. He was living with his parents (because they were taking over his place) and he was moving out. He/we lived with them for a year, he's still in it to this day, though his parents left a long time ago.

Always telling me what I should and shouldn't eat. I'm 5'7" and 115 pounds, and I'm size DD and he's always showing me plastic surgeons that do the best boob jobs so I can make them bigger. He was normal for four months, then told me he didn't want me hanging out with or speaking to other guys. He even would get annoyed when I'd talk to my mom or dad.

Long story short, when I started moving out, which has happened a million times, he became violent. Touching me, I'd ask him to stop, gently pushing him off me but he wouldn't and that's when he started strangling me. I've told people about him and they take his side, because he's such an upstanding member of the community.

He says guilt is a useless emotion and therefore feels none. He's broken six cell phones, and in turn I've broken things of his. He uses this as a way to twist it and say it's all my fault. He has every symptom on the sociopath checklist; I could go on and on. He got me a dog for my birthday and has started to use her as a tool to keep me home.

I've lost all my friends, rarely see family, but I'm so scared of life without him. I hate him, but every time I think about not having HIM in my life my chest hurts and it's hard to breathe. I've gone to the hospital because he choked me too long, and spit in my face and held me down and rubbed it in, and I can't or won't leave. Isn't that sick?

Initially I stayed because of the sex. Now I stay because I'm scared to be without him but also, I don't want him to be with someone else, although I think he might have cheated on me once. When I tell him all these things, he calls me insane and "such a victim" and that I'm "sandbagging him and that's all in the past."

I've called Women Helping Women, but your site was the most helpful so far and I don't know what to do. Everyone loves him; even the cops are his "braddahs." He's a college graduate; I only have high school (although I've gone to private schools my whole life) so he says no one would believe me, and they don't!

His ex told me he stalked her until she moved back to the mainland, and no one believed her either... I used to be really strong and confident, but now I can't leave the house without his approval of my outfit. I don't want him

9 control tactics in a classic story of sociopathic manipulation

to be with someone else, I don't want to be with him, but I don't want to be without him. He's becoming more and more negative and aggressive towards me, but I'm scared to leave and scared to stay.

I feel dumb, ugly, depressed, anxious, and trapped. He's drilled into my head for almost the whole two years that no other guys will date me or love me, and that they would only cheat on me. I know that's not true because I get asked out all the time, but now I'm terrified of being cheated on! What should I do? Oh also he has naked pics and video of me that he's threatened to release, even make money on.

Classic sociopath

This guy is a classic sociopath, employing every trick in the sociopath toolbox. He used the pity play to snag Chloe, with the story about his previous fiance being "mindf*cked" in therapy to leave him. Yeah, right—she probably fled because it was the only way to get rid of him.

Then the guy used sex to get his hooks into Chloe. As Dr. Liane Leedom explains, in normal people, intimate relations create bonds between them, and it worked with Chloe. These bonds, which are both psychological and hormonal, are Nature's way of holding the human race together for our own survival.

But it's possible for the bonds to become pathological. That can happen when someone—such as a sociopath—deliberately tries to bring another person under his or her control. Here's how this guy did it to Chloe:

1. Telling Chloe what she should eat and wear
2. Telling Chloe to get breast implants, even though it sounds like she has a fabulous figure
3. Isolating Chloe from her family and friends
4. Refusing to comply when she asks him not to touch her, then strangling her
5. Breaking cell phones—her way of contacting other people

6. Telling Chloe she is insane
7. Telling Chloe that no other man will have her
8. Twisting everything around so that all problems are Chloe's fault
9. Cycle of fear, anxiety, intimacy

Make no mistake—this is abuse. So what happens as a result? The guy creates fear and anxiety in Chloe. Fear and anxiety strengthen those attachment bonds, which started out being normal. What usually happens in these situations is that the victim turns to the abuser for relief from the fear and anxiety. The abuser then "forgives" the victim for "making him" act abusively. Then they have sex.

This cycle of fear-anxiety-intimacy keeps strengthening the psychological and hormonal attachment bond, actually rewiring the victim's brain. So now, even though Chloe knows the guy is bad news, it is almost impossible for her to get out of the relationship. This is apparent in the physical symptoms Chloe is showing just by thinking about leaving—her chest hurts and it's difficult to breathe.

Off the island

Yet Chloe must leave. She must find the strength to get away from the guy, even if it means voting herself off the island.

Leaving this sociopath will be much like breaking an addiction. This, too, is normal. As Dr. Leedom explains, the bonds created in these relationships use the same pathways in the brain as drug addictions. That's why Chloe has to go cold turkey with this guy, and why it will feel like withdrawal. The secret, as they say in recovery programs, it to take it one day at a time.

Chloe, do whatever you have to do to get out. Be prepared for the guy to pursue you, perhaps to the point of stalking, as he did with the previous woman. He may plead, beg, and even threaten. It's not because he loves you. It's because he doesn't want to lose his property. Because that's all you are to him—property.

The psychopath and our own self-image

"His online personal ad shows him as a clean-cut, athletic man with a friendly face, a sense of humor and a love for the outdoors. Many women would consider him a serious prospect, based on his ad. The problem is, Mike Andes is a convicted murderer."

A reader recently sent Lovefraud this news story about Prison Personals, produced by KATU in Portland, Oregon. It turns out that thousands of convicts are looking for love online.

Prisoners generally do not have access to the Internet. But apparently friends and family members can provide information to websites such as WriteAPrisoner.com, which then posts ads. Anyone who wants to respond to an ad — offering a gesture of friendship to someone behind bars — must send a reply via snail mail. According to KATU, the letters are flowing in.

Psychopaths in prison

The trouble is, many prisoners are looking for more than friendship. "Corrections officers know crafty convicts often prey on women," KATU reports. "They start by sending very innocent letters, then they'll ask for money, contraband, even help escaping." (The judge at the Patrick Giblin sentencing, which I attended on April 17, 2007, said Giblin was scamming women from jail.)

The fact is many prisoners are born manipulators. According to Dr. Robert Hare, about 25 percent of people in prison are psychopaths. In comparison, he says 1 percent of the general population are psychopaths. So anyone who writes to a prisoner has a one in four chance of contacting a con artist.

Lovefraud did hear from a woman who corresponded with a prisoner, then moved across the country to be with him when he was released from San Quentin. "He wrote beautiful, wonderful letters and sent hand-drawn cards," she said. "He said all the right things."

The woman found out, however, that the guy was saying the same things to his wife, whom he had promised to divorce. He was having sex with both women. Plus, he was still on drugs and still violent. The woman got away—but the wife stayed.

Targeting our self-image

How does this happen? How does someone fall in love with a guy in San Quentin?

I think part of the answer is that, as in online seduction, people fall in love with a fantasy. When a relationship is based on correspondence, they don't have direct information gleaned from a person's appearance and body language, so imagination is used to fill in the gaps.

But I also think there is a more important reason: Psychopaths use our own self-image against us.

J. Reid Meloy, Ph.D., writes that individuals who "consciously perceive themselves as being 'helpers' endowed with a special amount of altruism are exceedingly vulnerable to the affective simulation of the psychopath." In other words, if we perceive ourselves as kind-hearted, nonjudgmental, practicing Christian love or any variation of being a helper, psychopaths will play us to the max.

Any woman who writes to a prisoner out of compassion should be aware that a psychopathic prisoner will use her compassion against her.

Psychopaths will target other parts of our self-image is well. In my case, I saw myself as a reliable, competent and creative businesswoman. I was perfect prey for my psychopathic ex-husband with grandiose plans of becoming an entrepreneur. He complimented my talents, asked for my opinions, made me part of his projects, and wiped out my bank account.

The psychopath and our own self-image

In the end, we need to know psychopaths are out there. We also need to know ourselves, and recognize when someone is appealing to and flattering our own self-image.

10 terms to help you name your experience with a sociopath

One of the reasons why it's so difficult to explain what happens when you're involved with a sociopath is that you don't have the words.

Because of the general lack of awareness about personality disorders in society, and the lack of education about it, there is no generally accepted terminology to describe various aspects of the experience.

But descriptive language has evolved among online communities of survivors. Here is a vocabulary to help you name what you experienced. When you can name it, you can begin to recover from it.

1. Love Bombing

When sociopaths set about reeling you in, a key seduction strategy is love bombing. They shower you with attention and affection, want to be with you all the time, make you feel like the most important person in the world.

Not all sociopaths engage in love bombing, but many do. In fact, they may use the strategy even when a relationship isn't romantic, for example, flattering you if you're the boss.

2. Target

That would be you. Sociopaths don't look at you as a friend, colleague or romantic partner, they look at you as a target to be exploited.

10 terms to help you name your experience with a sociopath

When sociopaths meet you, they first evaluate you to determine if you have anything that they want, then figure out what your vulnerabilities are, and then use your vulnerabilities to get you to give them what they want.

3. Pity Play

Here's another key sociopathic seduction strategy: the pity play. Sociopaths try to make you feel sorry for them. They will tell you about their abusive childhood, or their cheating exes, or their dictatorial bosses. Of course, they lie a lot, so the stories may or may not be true.

The bottom line is that sociopaths intentionally use your empathy against you.

4. Jekyll and Hyde

This classic story of a man who turns from mild mannered to monster perfectly describes the behavior of sociopaths. One minute they love you; the next minute they hate you. They change like flipping a switch, and you have absolutely no idea what triggered it.

5. Gaslighting

In the 1944 movie called *Gaslight*, the villain intentionally tries to make his wife feel like she's losing her mind. If you watch the movie, you might wonder, who does that? Sociopaths do.

Sociopaths will tell you something, and then deny they ever said the words. They will hide objects and ask you what you did with them. They will ask you to do something, and then after you do it, ask you why you did it. Their goal is to make you doubt your own perceptions.

6. Flying Monkeys

Here's another movie reference from *The Wizard of Oz*. In this film, the flying monkeys do the bidding of the Wicked Witch of the West. Sociopaths often find their own flying monkeys — people who do their dirty work.

Some of these stooges gleefully go along with the sociopaths' schemes. But others are manipulated themselves, and have no idea that they are part of a plot. For example, sociopaths are capable of turning your own family members against you without them even knowing it.

7. Devalue and Discard

Once upon a time, you were the most important person in the world. But sooner or later, sociopaths are finished with you. They've taken all your love, money or whatever it was that they wanted, and you are totally depleted.

Now you are no longer useful, so the sociopaths rationalize that there is no reason to keep you around. You are discarded.

8. Smear Campaign

As your involvement with the sociopaths deteriorates, you may look for support among your friends and family. To your shock, nobody believes you.

Long before you realize that the sociopaths are toxic, they start undermining you with everyone you know. They wonder aloud about your mental or emotional stability. They tell outrageous stories about how you have wronged them — all lies. But they are so convincing that their accusations stick, and your support system is gone.

9. Hoovering

Finally, it's over. Either you escape from the sociopaths or you are discarded — either way, you are doing your best to move on.

Then they're back. The sociopaths are hoovering, as in the vacuum cleaner, trying to suck you back in. They tell you they realize they made a mistake, they treated you badly, they're sorry, they'll never do it again. Don't fall for it. It's just the same scam, the sequel.

10. No Contact

To escape and recover from sociopaths, the best strategy is No Contact. Get away and stay away. Do not see them, do not talk to them, do not text them, do not visit their Facebook page. Time and distance will help you clear the fog from your head and regain

10 terms to help you name your experience with a sociopath

your footing.

When No Contact isn't possible — perhaps if you share children with the sociopath — pursue Emotional No Contact. That means you understand what they are, that they will not change, and you no longer let them get under your skin.

How to protect yourself from sociopaths in 3 easy steps

Yes, you can protect yourself from having sociopaths come into your life and causing serious damage. I'm going to tell you how to do it in three easy steps:

Step 1 — Know that sociopaths exist

Millions of sociopaths live among us. I am not exaggerating that number.

I use the word "sociopath" as an umbrella term for four serious personality disorders. They are:

- Antisocial personality disorder/psychopathy
- Narcissistic personality disorder
- Borderline personality disorder
- Histrionic personality disorder

Although there are clinical differences among these disorders, there are many similarities. People who have these disorders are usually superficially charming. But they also tend to be exploitative, manipulative, deceitful, impulsive and lacking in empathy.

So how many people have these disorders? According to research by Randy A. Sansone, MD, and Lori A. Sansone, MD:

- Up to 4.5% of the population are antisocial or psychopaths
- Up to 6.2% of the population are narcissistic

- Up to 5.9% of the population are borderline
- Up to 3.8% of the population are histrionic

If you break the figures out by gender, about 12% of women and 16% of men may have these disorders. In the United States, that's approximately 30 million adults.

Plus, there are additional people who have antisocial, narcissistic, borderline or histrionic traits, but not the full disorder. Believe me, you don't want to get involved with them either.

Sociopaths can be male, female, old, young, rich, poor. They come from all races, religions, walks of life and segments of society.

Unfortunately, most of us are clueless about personality disorders, and how widespread they are. Anyone who is uninformed is vulnerable.

So this is the first step in protecting yourself: Know that sociopaths exist.

Step 2 — Know the warning signs of sociopathic behavior

As my research for my book, *Red Flags of Love Fraud: 10 signs you're dating a sociopath,* I conducted an Internet survey that was completed by more than 1,300 people. According to the survey results, most people see the warning signs of sociopathic behavior. They just don't know what the signs mean.

So what are the warning signs?

Charisma and charm. They're smooth talkers, always have an answer, never miss a beat. They seem to be very exciting.

Sudden soul mates. They figure out what you want, make themselves into that person, then tell you that your relationship was "meant to be."

Sexual magnetism. If you feel intense attraction, if your physical relationship is unbelievable, it may be their excess testosterone.

Love bombing. You're showered with attention and adoration. They want to be with you all the time. They call, text and e-mail constantly.

Blames others for everything. Nothing is ever their fault.

They always have an excuse. Someone else causes their problems.

Lies and gaps in the story. You ask questions, and the answers are vague. They lie. They tell stupid lies. They tell outrageous lies. They lie when they'd make out better telling the truth.

Intense eye contact. Call it the predatory stare. If you get a chill down your spine when they look at you, pay attention.

Moves fast to hook up. It's a whirlwind romance. They quickly proclaim their true love. They want to move in together or get married quickly.

Pity play. They appeal to your sympathy. They want you to feel sorry for their abusive childhood, psychotic ex, incurable disease or financial setbacks.

Jekyll and Hyde personality. One minute they love you; the next minute they hate you. Their personality changes like flipping a switch.

People who have one or two of these traits are not sociopaths. For example, someone can be charismatic and sexy without being disordered. For someone to be a sociopath, you need to see pretty much all of these symptoms.

If you do see this complete pattern, get the person out of your life.

For more description of each of these traits, read the *Red Flags of Love Fraud,* which is available in the Lovefraud Bookstore.

Step 3 — Trust your intuition

According to Gavin deBecker, author of *The Gift of Fear,* our intuition has evolved over millennia as an early warning system to protect us from danger.

So if you get a gut feeling that something is wrong with an individual, or you just know there is a problem, even if you can't put your finger on it, pay attention. That is your intuition warning you of danger.

Unfortunately, in Western society we are taught to value analysis and evidence over intuition. So even though you may have an internal siren blaring about someone, you may believe that you need proof of wrongdoing before taking steps to remove yourself from the situation.

This happens all the time. In my research for *Red Flags of Love Fraud,* I asked survey respondents whether they had an intuition or gut feeling early in a relationship that there was something wrong with the individual.

The result: 71% of people said yes. But most of them — 40% — went ahead with the relationship anyway.

Why? They doubted themselves. Or, they wanted to give the individual the benefit of the doubt. Or, they wanted to believe the best about the person.

Generally, when a person is bad news, your intuition will warn you. The important point is to act on the warning.

Awareness

Protecting yourself from sociopaths is a matter of awareness.

(The exception is when you're born into a family with sociopaths. Obviously you have no choice about who your relatives are, so the process of becoming aware and protecting yourself follows a different path.)

You may still meet a sociopath. After all, millions of them live among us, so it is likely that you will cross paths with a disordered person sooner or later.

But by knowing sociopaths exist, knowing the warning signs of sociopathic behavior, and paying attention to your intuition, you will protect yourself from inviting a sociopath into your life.

13 very early warning signs that your new partner may be a controller

The best way to escape a controlling or abusive relationship is to get out before you are emotionally hooked. But how can you tell when a new romantic interest may turn into a problem partner?

Here are 13 very early warning signs that may precede later abusive behavior.

1. Your new partner monopolizes your time

You are spending all your free time with your partner — perhaps even seeing him or her every day. If you spend any time with someone else, your partner seems hurt, annoyed or even angry.

2. Your new partner calls or texts constantly

You may get calls and texts 24/7 — even if you are also spending a lot of time with this person. If you don't respond immediately and your partner demands to know why — well, consider this a serious warning.

3. Your new partner plays for your sympathy

Your new partner may talk about an abusive childhood, scheming boss or treacherous previous love interest. This warning sign is especially relevant if he or she tells you that a previous partner was cheating, abusive or mentally unbalanced (very common accusations for abusers).

4. Your partner overreacts to a trivial or nonexistent slight

He or she becomes angry or sullen over nothing at all, or accuses you of saying or doing something that simply didn't happen.

5. Your partner is worked up, and says it's your fault

During debate, discussion or argument, your partner is combative and says, "You made me say it," or "You made me do it," or, "You made me crazy," or something like that. If your partner blames you for his or her behavior, this is a classic controller technique.

6. Early on, your partner buys you extravagant gifts

You've only been dating a short time, but he or she buys you an expensive gift, like jewelry or electronics or offers you money, and it just feels inappropriate. This may be an attempt to make you feel indebted.

7. You see a sudden flash of nastiness that seems out of character

Maybe it's not directed towards you — perhaps your partner is rude to a waiter. If your partner has been treating you like gold, and suddenly you see a mean streak, well, perhaps the person's mask has slipped, and revealed what's behind it.

8. "Where did that come from?"

Your partner says or does something negative, and your immediate reaction is, "Huh? Where did that come from?" If you are shocked for any reason, do not overlook the incident.

9. All your interactions are on the your partner's terms

You spend time at your partner's house, with your partner's friends and family, doing what your partner wants to do. You never seem to get to what you want to do. If your partner does finally agree to what you want, he or she makes the experience so miserable that you never ask again.

10. Your partner starts to criticize you

In the beginning your partner continuously told you how wonderful you are. Now, he or she is finding things about you to criticize, although the criticisms may be presented in the context of "helping" or "for your own good." Remember, romantic partners are supposed to be supportive.

11. Your partner physically assaults you, even if it doesn't hurt

This is major, major, major. If your partner shoves, hits, scratches or chokes you, even lightly, you should assume that he or she is testing you. Your partner may claim it was an accident, he or she didn't mean it, it will never happen again. Actually, your partner may be taking the first steps towards training you to tolerate physical abuse.

12. Your partner pushes your sexual boundaries

Your partner may make suggestions or demands that you just find uncomfortable, all for more "fantasy" or "excitement." Well, it may be just the beginning of uncomfortable demands, and the depravity of the demands may escalate.

13. You feel drained

Perhaps your partner is being demanding, although the demands are hidden in the context of wanting to spend so much time with you. Perhaps you feel like you are constantly defending yourself. Whatever the reason, this relationship leaves you feeling drained. Keep in mind that controllers suck the life out of you.

What should you think? What should you do?

You may be inclined to interpret overly attentive behaviors to mean that your new partner is really smitten with you. Or if you see some nastiness, you may feel like you should cut the person some slack, because we all have bad days, and we all have wounds and baggage.

So how do you know if one of these episodes is an aberration, or a warning?

13 very early warning signs that your new partner may be a controller

Listen to your instincts. If you have a nagging intuition or a bad feeling that there is something wrong with this person or the involvement, and you also see these behaviors, consider yourself warned.

More importantly, act on the warning and end your involvement. The sooner you get out, the safer you will be.

Sociopaths target our dreams

Lovefraud received the following email. In it, I felt like I was reading a rerun of my experience.

    I was involved with one of those 1 to 4% sociopaths/scammers you've outlined in your website.
    I lost everything. Long story — you already know it — he was so charming — the love of my life — kind generous, giving, very sexy in and out of bed.
    Anyways, it's been just over 3 yrs (I was only with him 2 + yrs with a 3-month breakup period. Yep I took him back. Call me a LOSER now and hit the delete button — Wait, please don't — and I'm living in a mobile home park. Not any of the three properties I had on a golf course. Sold two of them and the third is heading for foreclosure. Put all the money 250K+ into a condo in Mexico and took loans out on my condo that I had paid off while I was selling new homes from '95 -'05) the year I met him — to pay for "our dream" — live in Mexico.
    I had an offer letter to work for the Four Seasons (selling luxury time shares — the interviews were long and the background check very extensive — I passed) and that would help pay the mortgage on the 3,000 sq. ft. beachfront condo WE bought — none of his money till he made some payments — And my job would hopefully cover his expenses of running his dream job of being a charter cap-

tain on a boat that we would lease from the person we bought the condo from — OMG — Thanks for listening. — I need a support group to go to— but I'd rather just be one-on-one and I've been to the therapists — they all (so far) just watch the clock and tell me stuff I already know.

Been extremely depressed — always suffered depression but was able to work and acquire my homes. Then, all of his promises and "deals" shot all my $$ and savings out the window — at a very high speed mind you.

How long does it take to get on with life?

My friends, which are fewer nowadays, say get over it and move on. But, I considered myself to be somewhat "street smart" — And so I continue to beat myself up for the horrific financial things I did and the mess I'm in — I know I need to accept some of the blame — but — he had the plan — didn't know his plan — and went along with the Love sick person inside of me —finally, my ugh, prince had come — yada, yada, yada.

At the end (two weeks before our big move to start our new "fabulous" lives together — I finally confronted him about his 150K in credit card debt. I have no idea — why I didn't run his credit before that close to our move — other than he was always paying for everything, including ALWAYS having to upgrade our flights to first class, etc — I thought he was just spoiling me — as he told me time and again — I deserved to be treated like a lady and he was going to be the one to do that — and claiming to pay off his cards monthly with his construction job.

By the way, yes he allowed me to run his credit one night when he was having one of his daily 6 Bud Lights. I'd gone to bed early — he came home beyond plastered, woke me up from a sound sleep and poured beer all over me — threw me to the ground and threatened to kill me ("Do you want me to kill you now?") I responded two-fold. "Why are you wasting a beer?" and "No, I'd like to make it to my 43rd b-day."

I called the police after he got up from holding me by

my neck to the ground of our bedroom floor — I called a cab, as I'd already sold my sports car (as it wouldn't have been too practical in Mexico) — stayed in a motel for 2 weeks — next day called some movers and moved all my stuff to a storage — then after two weeks in "hiding" — because I was afraid he'd go to my girlfriends homes looking for me. I stayed with a girlfriend until the tenants in my condo found a new place to move.

Sorry for rambling on — to repeat — it's been just over 3 yrs — and I can remember everything like it was yesterday.

How long till I regain my life? I'm sure the answer is in ME — maybe a lobotomy? Please advise or let me know that I still have a life that's worth living. I'll be 46 in Feb — He'll be turning 60 next yr.

Insidious tactic

This reader described in living color probably the most insidious tactic in the sociopathic arsenal: They target our dreams.

What better way to draw us in than to promise to make our deepest desires come true? How can we resist someone who wants what we want, and seemingly has the capacity to achieve it?

And how do the sociopaths know what we want? They ask us, and we tell them.

It happens early in the relationship, under the guise of "getting to know each other." It goes something like this:

"So," the sociopath asks, with pitch-perfect sincerity, "what do you really want in life?"

"I want a family before I get too old," we reply. (Or, "I want to live on the beach on a tropical island." Or, "I want to send my kids to a top college." Or, "I want to retire while I'm still young enough to enjoy it.")

"That's what I want," the sociopath replies, with a touch of feigned surprise. "We have so much in common. We must be meant for each other."

Painful betrayal

Dreams explain one reason why the betrayal of the sociopath

is so painful. Not only have they manipulated us, deceived us and stolen from us, but they used our own most treasured dreams to do it.

We have lost not only our love, money, time, home, and whatever else they have taken. We've lost our dreams. And that hurts.

Then, of course, comes the self-criticism. Why did we believe the sociopath? Why did we wait so long to check them out? Why didn't we listen to people who warned us? Why didn't we listen to ourselves?

Why? Because we wanted our dreams to come true.

It's a brilliant tactic on the part of the predators. They use our dreams to hook us, and then because of our dreams, we don't want to let go.

Recovery

So how, as this reader asks, do you move on in life? "I'm sure the answer is in me," she writes.

She is right. A lobotomy is not necessary, but a "pain-ectomy" is. We have real, true, genuine pain because of what the sociopath did. In my opinion, we can't analyze away the pain, or wish it away. Pain is emotional, and the only way to release it is emotional. We have to allow ourselves to experience it.

The only way out of the pain is through it.

This isn't pretty. In my case, I spent a lot of time crying. To get out my anger, I imagined the con man's face in a pillow, and beat it as hard as I could. Because our dreams were damaged, the pain goes deep, and releasing it is a process. We get rid of some, and more rises to take its place.

Eventually, however, we get to the point where we've cried all the tears and released all the anger. We get to the point of acceptance. Something awful happened, we had a part in it, but it's time to move on.

Then we learn something about dreams. Dreams are linked to expectations, and expectations have a down side. Sometimes, if our expectations aren't met, we feel like we've failed. Or, expectations blind us to other opportunities that may come our way. Because the new opportunities do not match our expectations, we don't even see them.

Maybe we have to give up our original dreams. But that doesn't mean there will never be dreams again. Perhaps something better, and more fulfilling, will come along, and because we are no longer looking to make a particular dream come true, we'll see the new opportunity.

7 fake reasons why sociopaths seem so romantic

People who have been in a relationship with a sociopath frequently say that they were swept off their feet in a whirlwind romance. But what, exactly, does that mean?

Here are six strategies that sociopaths employ to make you fall for them — hard and fast — and why the romance is not at all what it seems to be.

1. Sociopaths want to be with you, or in contact with you, all the time

They call for dates. They want to hang out. They book your calendar weeks in advance. They may go to great lengths to see you — driving long distances or booking a flight. You may feel overwhelmed with the attention, and believe that your new romantic interest is just so smitten with you that he or she can't stand to be apart.

Of course, sometimes they don't show up. When that happens, they always have an excuse — they suddenly had to work late, or their mother had a serious accident — when the real reason is that they are also pursuing someone else.

If they can't be physically with you, they keep in touch, calling, texting and emailing constantly. Again, you interpret this as a sign of romantic interest. The truth is, this is the beginning of keeping tabs on you — in other words, establishing control.

2. Romantic texts and emails

The messages are mushier than anything ever produced by

Hallmark cards. Or perhaps they are erotic, making you feel like the sexiest person alive. You may have never heard such sentiments from a love interest, and believe that the touching, exciting words reflect his or her true feelings. After all, who would lie about such things?

Well, sociopaths do. Often, they don't even write the messages. Two Nigerian scammers likely used messages out of a book called, *For You, My Soul Mate,* to steal £1.6 million from a British woman.

My sociopathic ex-husband, James Montgomery, stole an erotic story written by one of his partners, changed the names, and sent it to me — and multiple other women. In fact, he had a whole file full of poems and other pithy sayings that he recycled among his new targets.

From the sociopath's point of view, if it works once, do it again.

3. Shower you with gifts

Sociopaths may shower you with gifts, sometimes without an occasion — "just because I was thinking of you." This isn't unusual when you're being courted. But where, exactly, did the gift come from? And was it purchased just for you?

Ladies — beware of the beau who slips up behind you and fastens a necklace around your neck. When jewelry doesn't arrive in a gift box, there's a good chance it was stolen from another woman.

After discovering that James Montgomery was cheating on me, I met with one of his other victims. She pulled all kinds of jewelry out of her bag. "Is any of this yours?" she asked.

She had some of my bracelets that I didn't even know were missing. One necklace Montgomery had given her wasn't mine — but I had one just like it. Apparently when he did shop, he shopped for all his women at once.

4. They're quickly willing to say, "I love you"

The purpose of dating is to find a romantic partner. If you're like most people, you've had your heart broken once or multiple times, so you're cautious about revealing your feelings.

Sociopaths, however, quickly proclaim love, telling you that you're the person they've been waiting for all their lives. They immediately want to move in together, get married and start a family. They paint a glorious verbal picture of your life together, complete with everything you ever wanted and a white picket fence.

You would never say such things unless you meant it. So you assume that the sociopaths mean it.

They don't. In fact, they don't know what love is. But they do know that if they say, "I love you," they get what they want.

Frequently, once you're committed to them, the "I love you's" stop.

5. Sex, sex, sex

Sociopaths usually push for a physical relationship quickly. In fact, I've heard from numerous people who met the sociopaths online that they had sex on the first date. Many people also say that sex with the sociopath was the best they ever had — at least in the beginning of the relationship.

Sociopaths may tell you that you are irresistible and they can't get enough of you, but the truth is that they are simply hardwired for sex. They want a lot of sex, in a lot of ways. They have boundless energy, no inhibitions and they indulge frequently.

So even if you're with the sociopath multiple times a day — well, don't assume that you are the only partner.

6. The grand gesture

Sociopaths sometimes pull out all the stops to proclaim their love. They'll spend a lot of money, or put on a big display, often in front of an audience.

For example, I knew of a woman who ditched a sociopath because he was borrowing money and not paying it back. The sociopath, who was very handsome, got all dressed up in a suit, bought a massive bouquet of roses, and showed up at the office tower where she worked.

The guy called her and asked her to come down to the atrium. She was reluctant, but he talked her into it. Then, right there in the atrium, in front of dozens of professionals, he got on his knee, presented the roses, and proposed. The woman accepted — much to her later regret.

7. Every romantic fantasy

When a sociopath is focused on you, showering you with attention and affection, you may feel like every romantic fantasy you ever had is being fulfilled. Unfortunately, it's all fake.

Sociopaths target you because you have something that they want. Every romantic gesture has an ulterior motive.

That's why it's so important to protect yourself. Here's how:

1. Know that sociopaths exist and that they are everywhere.
2. Know the Red Flags of Love Fraud
3. Trust your instincts. If you get a gut feeling that something is wrong, it probably is.

Love, sex, your brain and sociopaths

Ever since the beginning of recorded history, humans have been trying to understand and explain the mysteries of love and sex. Over the past few decades, scientists started using specialized equipment to measure physical arousal by attaching devices to private parts. More recently, they've been observing the most important romantic organ in the human body—the brain.

Forbes Magazine wrote about the research of Andreas Bartels, Ph.D., at the Imperial College of London. Bartels used a functional magnetic resonance imaging (fMRI) machine, which can capture images of brain activity, to pinpoint the areas of the brain that are activated by love.

Bartles did a study of 17 people who were madly in love. He had the test subjects look at photos of platonic friends and of their loved ones while he observed activity in their brains. The resulting images clearly showed that certain sections of the brain are stimulated by love.

The scientist then did another study to observe the brains of mothers looking at their infants. The images showed that exactly the same areas of the brain were stimulated by maternal love, except for an area in the hypothalamus in the base of the brain that seems to be linked to sexual arousal.

The conclusion, therefore, is that specific areas of the brain light up at the prospect of love.

Bartels also noticed something else: When the test subjects were feeling love, certain areas of the brain were turned off. The scans showed that three regions of the brain generally associated with moral judgment go dim.

Chemistry of love

Then there's the chemistry of love. Helen Fisher, Ph.D., a professor at Rutgers University, has written that three networks in the brain, and their associated neurotransmitters, are associated with love. They are:

- **Lust**—the craving for sexual gratification, which is linked to testosterone in both men and women.
- **Romantic attraction**—the elation and yearning of new love, which is linked to the natural stimulants dopamine and norepinephrine, and low activity in serotonin.
- **Attachment**—the calm emotional union with a long-term partner, which is linked to oxytocin and vasopressin.

Fisher also did a study using fMRI technology. She scanned the brains of 40 men and women who were wildly in love. When these people gazed at photos of their beloved, the scans showed increased activity in the areas of the brain that produce dopamine. This neurochemical is associated with feelings of excessive energy, elation, focused attention and motivation to win rewards.

Dopamine, by the way, is also the neurotransmitter associated with addiction.

Effects of arousal

Research has also proven what we've probably all experienced—sexual arousal can make us throw caution to the winds.

In another study using fMRI technology, Dr. Ken Maravilla of the University of Washington found that sexual arousal dims down the parts of the brain that control inhibition and, perhaps, moral judgment.

"These are things that keep you in line, and in arousal they may become less active, allowing you to become more aroused,"

Maravilla said, as quoted by Wired Magazine.

In a paper called, *The Heat of the Moment: The Effect on Sexual Arousal on Sexual Decision Making,* Dan Ariely, of the Massachusetts Institute of Technology, and George Lowenstein, of Carnegie Mellon University, documented that being sexually turned on affected the judgment of college-aged men. (Well, duh!)

Specifically, Ariely and Lowenstein found that, "the increase in motivation to have sex produced by sexual arousal seems to decrease the relative importance of other considerations, such as behaving ethically toward a potential sexual partner or protecting oneself against unwanted pregnancy or sexually transmitted disease."

But another of their findings was, "people seem to have only limited insight into the impact of sexual arousal on their own judgments and behavior." In other words, most of us don't appreciate how strong the sex urges are, and how they can make us do things that perhaps we shouldn't be doing.

Sociopathic seduction

So let's look at all this information in the context of our relationships with sociopaths.

Two of the main strategies that sociopaths use to snare us are love and sex. They emphatically proclaim their love and consciously seduce us into having sex. So what happens?

- Love causes specific areas of the brain light up, and at the same time, areas associated with morals and judgment go dim.
- The areas of the brain that produce dopamine become active, and dopamine is related to addiction.
- Sexual arousal dims the parts of the brain responsible for inhibition and judgment that might prevent us from making bad choices.
- We don't recognize the impact that sexual urges have on our judgment and behavior.

Dr. Helen Fisher writes that the three primary brain systems associated with love evolved over the ages to play different roles in courtship, mating, reproduction and parenting. They are Nature's way of ensuring the survival of the human species.

Sociopaths convincingly proclaim their enduring love and their sexual desire for us. Not realizing the pervasive deceit of these predators, we believe that they love us. We have sex with them, and the sex is great. Many Lovefraud readers have been amazed at the sociopath's sexual appetite and prowess.

Therefore, sociopaths hijack our brain through our feelings of love and the bonds of sex. In their seductions, they turn the natural psychological and chemical functions of our brains against us.

8 reasons why we can't see what's wrong with the sociopath

"I could smell the smoke, but I could never find the fire." That's how one Lovefraud reader explained her experience with a sociopath. She sensed that something was terribly wrong, but could never figure out what it was.

Other Lovefraud readers described the same situation this way, "I knew something was off, but I couldn't put my finger on it."

Why is this? Why can't we see what later turns out to be massive lying, exploitation and betrayal?

Following are eight reasons why we may suspect that something about the sociopath isn't right, but we don't identify it.

1. We don't know sociopaths exist

No one tells us that 12% of women and 16% of men — about 30 million adults in the U.S. — are seriously disordered. How can we watch out for trouble that we don't know about?

2. We don't know the warning signs of sociopathic behavior

Yes, there are distinct patterns of disordered behavior — I catalogue them in my book, *Red Flags of Lovefraud — 10 signs you're dating a sociopath*. But no one tells us them either.

3. Sociopaths seem so normal

Even if we had heard about sociopaths, we believe they're

criminals, drug dealers or serial killers. Who knew they could disguise themselves as pillars of the community?

4. We don't know the sociopaths are lying

Sociopaths lie like they breathe. They are totally convincing. And humans can spot lies only 53% of the time. We don't stand a chance.

5. The sociopath is saying, "I love you"

We're being told how wonderful, smart, talented and beautiful we are. Of course, we want to believe it — so we also believe everything else the sociopath tells us.

6. The sociopath always has a believable explanation

On the few occasions where we do question the sociopaths, they have a reasonable excuse or explanation.

7. We try asking questions — but stop

After a few attempts at disputing the sociopaths — and being told we are paranoid, bipolar or untrusting — we learn it is better to keep our mouths shut.

8. Everyone else thinks the sociopath is wonderful

Friends, acquaintances and co-workers all think the sociopaths are terrific. If we are the only people with doubts, we assume the problem is us.

How sociopaths intentionally mess with your mind

I talk to a lot of people who are, or have been, involved with sociopaths. Time and time again they tell me, "I feel like I'm losing my mind."

This is exactly how sociopaths want you to feel. Why? Because if you are confused and unsure of yourself, you are more pliable. You are easier to control, and what sociopaths want is to control you.

So how do they mess with your mind?

Lies from hello to goodbye

First of all, they lie.

Now, this may not sound all that terrible, because we all lie from time to time. But normal people lie to get out of trouble or spare someone's feelings. Sociopaths lie because they have an agenda.

The lying starts at the very beginning of your involvement. How? Sociopaths misrepresent their reasons for even talking to you. They begin their interactions with you as colleagues, friends, neighbors, or if you meet through a dating site, as potential romantic partners. They do not identify themselves as predators who are looking to exploit you.

Think about how damaging this is. You are under the impression that you are building a friendship, work relationship or romance. Sociopaths, unbeknownst to you, view you as a target. So even if you are moving forward slowly, you are behaving according to one set of rules, and the sociopaths have a different set of rules — or no rules at all.

The entire foundation of your involvement with the sociopaths is a deception — and they keep the deception going from beginning to end.

Catching the lies

Sooner or later, you probably catch some of the lies. When you question the sociopaths, they completely deny whatever you discovered, become enraged that you even questioned them, and turn things around so that it's all your fault.

All of this is designed to make you doubt yourself.

The sociopaths act hurt, indignant or righteous, saying something like, "I would never do that." You are floored by the intensity of the denials.

This leads to cognitive dissonance — discomfort caused by holding two or more contradictory beliefs, ideas or values at the same time. The psychological theory is that humans strive for internal consistency, so one or the other of the contradictory beliefs has to go.

Here's what happens:

1. You discover discrepancies in the sociopaths' stories.
2. The sociopaths vehemently deny your observation; in fact, they accuse you of disloyalty or paranoia for even questioning them.
3. You believe that you and the sociopaths are on the same page about the nature of your involvement — you don't realize that their agenda is to exploit you.
4. Your observation does not match the sociopaths' strenuous denials. You believe your involvement with the sociopath is authentic, so the only way you can resolve the cognitive dissonance is to accept that you must be wrong.
5. That means you aren't perceiving life correctly, which means you're losing your mind.

Telling you that you're crazy

This pattern repeats time and time again. You discover a lie, and the sociopaths cover it with another lie. You say the sociopaths broke a promise, and they deny that the promise was ever made. As you become more and more frustrated and upset, the sociopaths start talking about your "mental state."

At first they may express gentle concern about your "forgetfulness" or "paranoia." They may suggest that you seek counseling. If you buy the idea that they are right and you are losing it, and actually take steps to "get help," well, to the sociopaths, this is all they need to go in for the kill.

They tell you, your family, your friends and your employer that you are mentally unstable. They may drag you to a psychiatrist and convince the doctor to give you drugs. They may try to get you involuntarily committed to a psychiatric facility.

You, constantly being told that you're unbalanced, crazy or in the early stages of dementia, start to believe it.

How to escape and recover

Here's how to recover yourself: Learn the characteristics and tactics of sociopaths — Lovefraud has plenty of articles that will help you.

This will help you to understand what happened:

1. You were targeted
2. The sociopath took advantage of you very human characteristics, such as trust and empathy.
3. Your perceptions were right all along.

You are not losing your mind. If you feel disoriented, you are having a normal reaction to being involved with a sociopath. Your entire involvement was based on deception from the get-go, and the sociopaths' mind games were intentional.

7 reasons not to have sex with a sociopath

Many people — both men and women — have told me that sex with a sociopath is the best they ever had. It was exciting, wild and plentiful. They never felt so desired.

Well, there are reasons for this.

First of all, both male and female sociopaths are hardwired for sex. They crave excitement and stimulation. They have high levels of testosterone, which makes them aggressively pursue sex. They start young and engage frequently. They have a lot of desire, a lot of energy and a lot of practice.

So sex with a sociopath is out of this world — at least in the beginning of an involvement. But there are serious downsides:

1. Sociopaths cheat

Sociopaths are promiscuous — it's one of the traits of the disorder. They start young and engage frequently. What they really want in their sex lives is variety, including a variety of partners. No matter how they may proclaim that they've changed, that you're the person they've been waiting for forever and they'll never need to look at another partner — well, sociopaths also lie a lot, and that's one of their biggest lies. If you want a monogamous relationship, you will never get it with a sociopath.

2. Sociopaths will push your boundaries

Sociopaths want excitement, stimulation and variety. They also get bored easily. So once your novelty as a new partner has worn off, they'll want to shake up their love life, perhaps by engaging in practices that you find uncomfortable. They'll make suggestions, and if you resist, they'll lay on the guilt trip — "if you really loved me, you would do it." They'll chip away at your protests, until one day you may find yourself doing things that you once thought were degrading.

3. Sociopaths use sex to manipulate you

Sociopaths target you because you have something that they want, and it may not be sex. Perhaps you have money, a nice home, social or business connections. Sociopaths know that if they can hook you sexually, you are easier to manipulate. So they take you to bed, and then press for what they really want. This is especially dangerous if you are married to someone else, work for the same organization or hold a prominent position — all of which would make you susceptible to blackmail.

4. You'll get addicted to the relationship

Sociopaths hijack the human bonding system. Love bonds are established in the beginning of the involvement, when sociopaths shower you with attention and sex. Sexual intimacy floods your body with oxytocin, a hormone and neurotransmitter that is the glue that holds people together. The more sex you have, the more you want the relationship. You can become addicted to the relationship, which makes it difficult to escape, even when you know something is wrong with the person.

5. You'll catch a sexually transmitted disease

Sociopaths are promiscuous. They are also reckless. And they want their stimulation. Taken together, this means they often don't want to use protection. In a survey of Lovefraud readers, 20 percent said they acquired an STD from the sociopath. In some cases, the sociopaths knew they were HIV positive, but continued to have unprotected sex, intentionally infecting multiple partners.

6. Sociopaths may lie about sexual orientation

Some sociopaths are straight, some are gay, and some are

neither straight nor gay — they'll have sex with anyone. In a Lovefraud survey, 18.5 percent of respondents said their sociopathic partners lied about their sexual orientation. Why? It's not necessarily because they were gay and still in the closet. More likely, they were looking for variety, or you have something that they want, and they are using sex as a tool to manipulate you.

7. You could end up with a pregnancy

Many sociopaths — both male and female — use pregnancy to trap their partners. Having a child with a sociopath is a nightmare. First of all, it gives the sociopath an opportunity to manipulate you for the rest of your life. Secondly, and more importantly, sociopathy is highly genetic. Your child may inherit a predisposition to the disorder, and grow up to be a sociopath also. I know of many parents who had to accept that their children are disordered, and it's heartbreaking.

Sex with a sociopath may be thrilling in the moment, but it could result in serious, life-changing consequences. If you at all suspect that your charming, exciting new love interest is disordered, don't go to bed with this person, and exit the involvement as soon as you can.

Sociopaths and their multiple simultaneous manipulation strategies

Lovefraud received the following question from a reader who was looking for validation:

> My father was a nut job and so was my husband and now I am dating one — a psychopath. I just had this question —
> Do these men act like they do not want you around and push you away and make you feel so sad for them — making you feel like you failed them somehow — never do enough — and then suddenly you find yourself begging them to show you how much better you can do for them?
> I am sure the answer is yes — but I guess I just need confirmation.

This reader, in one sentence, listed four different manipulation tactics employed by sociopaths:

1. Acting like they don't want you and pushing you away
2. Making you feel sad for them
3. Making you feel like you failed them
4. Making you feel like you need to prove yourself to them

All of these are typical sociopathic behaviors. In fact, items 2 and 3 are alternate descriptions for some of the Red Flags of Love Fraud.

Let's take a look at these strategies individually.

1. Acting like they don't want you and pushing you away

In the *Red Flags of Love Fraud,* I list warning signs such as "love bombing," which is showering the target with attention and affection, and "moving fast to hook up." Sociopaths often pursue you relentlessly, sometimes snagging you through sheer persistence.

Then, suddenly, they act like they are no longer interested in you.

Because of the neurochemistry of how romantic love affects your brain — it's addictive — this has the effect of making you want the sociopath even more. Sociopaths pursue you, then push you away, then pursue you, then push you away. With each manipulative cycle, the bond that you feel for the person gets stronger and stronger.

2. Making you feel sad for them

This is Red Flag #9 — "The pity play." Sociopaths will tell you sob stories about their abusive childhood, crazy ex, overbearing boss, chronic illnesses — anything to get you to feel sorry for them.

In her book, *The Sociopath Next Door,* Dr. Martha Stout wrote:

> "The most reliable sign, the most universal behavior of unscrupulous people is not directed, as one might imagine, at our fearfulness. It is, perversely, an appeal to our sympathy."

The stories sociopaths tell are often highly exaggerated or even complete fabrications, but they tell them so well that you are manipulated into believing them.

3. Making you feel like you failed them

This is Red Flag #5 — "Blames others for everything." Sociopaths will blame anybody but themselves for their problems.

Sociopaths and their multiple simultaneous manipulation strategies

When you become romantically involved with a sociopath, sooner or later you will likely become the prime target for blaming.

What's even worse is that you likely never did any of the actions or omissions that you are being accused of. Or, if you are guilty of a misunderstanding or oversight, the sociopath blows it way out of proportion, as if some minor incident were a federal crime.

No matter — the sociopath has manipulated you to be on the defensive. This leads to the next tactic:

4. Making you feel like you need to prove yourself to them

This is the most insidious manipulation tactic that our reader pointed out, because the sociopath uses you against yourself. And surprisingly, the sociopath may manipulate your strengths as well as your weaknesses.

For example, if you are intelligent, or accomplished, or caring, the sociopath may imply, or even tell you outright, that you are not intelligent, accomplished, or caring enough. The result — you work harder to prove that you are.

The more you work to prove yourself, the more invested you become in the relationship — which strengthens the sociopath's grip on you.

Multiple manipulation strategies

The true significance of the Lovefraud reader's question is something she implied but did not ask directly. By mentioning four different ways in which the sociopath treated her, she captured the essence of what makes dealing with them so confusing:

They employ multiple manipulation strategies simultaneously.

This is why you feel so confused and off-balance. Although you don't realize it, everything has an agenda. Nothing the sociopath says or does is real or authentic. Everything is about pulling you into the web, and keeping you there.

Unfortunately, it works.

10 signs you're addicted to loving a cheater

Editor's note: All of the following still apply if your partner is a woman.

You know he's seeing another woman. Or perhaps you ARE the other woman. Why can't you let him go?

You discover your man is cheating. You know he's bad for you. Your friends tell you to dump him, but the truth is, you still want him.

If the pull is unbearably strong, maybe it's not love that you feel—but addiction. Do you do any of the following? (Be honest!)

1. You confront him about the calls in his phone from other women. He comes up excuses, you know they're lame—but you accept them anyway.
2. He says that it's your fault that he cheated on you, and you agree with him.
3. You keep telling yourself that if you could just be more loving, patient, sexy—(fill in the blank)—he will make you his one-and-only.
4. You apologize to him for things you didn't do or say.
5. You tell him it's over and storm out, only to call or text him, begging to get back together. This happens time and time again.
6. You keep trying to prove that you're better than the other woman (or women).
7. You go overboard trying to help him, even though he treats you badly.

8. When your friends and family question his behavior, you make excuses for him.
9. You stalk him—in real life and online.
10. He promises that this time will be different and he really will end it with her. You make yourself believe him. Again.

How does this happen?

First of all, understand this: All romantic love is addictive.

Anyone who falls madly in love behaves just like an addict, says Dr. Helen E. Fisher, a biological anthropologist at Rutgers University.

In her scientific articles, she explains the similarities between lovers and addicts:

- You are both intensely focused on your reward—either your lover or the drug.
- You both feel mood swings, craving, obsession and compulsion.
- You both experience distortion of reality, emotional dependence, personality changes, risk-taking and loss of self-control.

Romantic love can be a constructive addiction when your love is returned, Dr. Fisher says. But if your love isn't returned, if you are rejected, the addiction can be highly destructive.

Dr. Fisher explains your first reaction to rejected love is "protest"—you obsessively try to win back your partner. You may even feel more passionately in love than when you were together.

Why? Because you have bonded to your lover.

All love is about bonding—the psychological and emotional attachment that you feel towards him.

The psychological bond forms in the beginning of the relationship, when you feel the giddy pleasure of a new romance.

What happens when you discover your man is cheating on you? You may be angry. But you may also feel fear and anxiety about possibly losing your relationship.

Surprisingly, this doesn't drive you away from your lover. According to Dr. Liane Leedom, associate professor of counseling and psychology at the University of Bridgeport, fear and anxiety actually strengthen the psychological bond that you feel for him.

When the guy is a cheater, this becomes a vicious cycle:

1. In the beginning, before you knew of his deception, the pleasure of your new romance created the psychological bond.
2. He cheats and you feel fear and anxiety, which strengthens the bond.
3. You kiss and make up, which strengthens the bond again.
4. He takes you on a rollercoaster of cheating and reuniting. With each go-round, the psychological bond you feel gets stronger and stronger.

The vicious cycle of cheating and reuniting could lead to a "trauma bond."

Some cheaters aren't just guys who can't make up their minds. Some cheaters are exploiters.

"Exploitative relationships create betrayal bonds," says Dr. Patrick J. Carnes in his book called, *The Betrayal Bond*. Also described as a trauma bond, this occurs when you bond with someone who is destructive to you.

Trauma bonds, Dr. Carnes explains, are addictive. You feel a compulsion to continue the relationship, despite the adverse consequences. You are obsessed with the relationship.

If you recognize yourself in this description, you are probably already aware that your involvement with this man is not healthy.

So what do you do? You treat it like an addiction. You "go on the wagon" by breaking off the relationship and having No Contact with this man.

This may seem daunting—how can you possibly cut him out of your life? The answer is to take it one day at a time, just like in a 12-step program. And if you need support, seek competent help.

Are these warning signs that I'm involved with a sociopath?

Editor's note: Lovefraud received the following letter from a reader whom we'll call "Cassandra18."

I've been a longtime reader of your website and wanted to thank you for what a valuable tool it is. I figured, I'd finally write in with a question of my own and I was hoping for some feedback from you.

So, the thing is, I have a propensity to date very selfish, controlling people and two of my past relationships have been with verifiable sociopaths.

Most recently, I have been in and out of a relationship with a man I used to work with. Something keeps telling me that something is off about him but I can't pinpoint it.

Some of the warning signs that have happened while with him:

He love bombed me in the beginning and brought me flowers and Starbucks and constantly texted and called. He also wrote me several love letters and left notes on my car. He told me I was his soul mate and poured the compliments on.

On our first date he "forgot" his wallet and I paid. He also "forgot" his wallet when we went to Target and I paid for his son's birthday presents.

He had a horrible relationship with his ex-wife and he told me how one morning he went to pick up his kids and she threw coffee in his face. I met his wife and she was nice and seemed like a good mom to his kids. I don't know what he did to make her so upset to throw coffee at him. I also saw a text from her to him saying he almost forced her into bankruptcy and that he didn't pay for anything for his kids.

He had a bad tendency to talk down to people and over them. He would literally talk over me several times while I was talking.

He had anger issues.

He had me help serve beer for a fundraiser when he knew I was an alcoholic.

He had an odd relationship with 2 elderly women, one of whom had severe dementia. The other one's nephew had to block him from calling her and accused him of trying to take advantage of her.

He eventually got fired and my boss told me that he had been embezzling money.

At work he had a hot head and yelled at one of our coworkers.

When we would get in fights he would text my boss who was his friend and he disclosed all of our personal issues.

The list goes on and on...

What are your thoughts? Does he sound like a sociopath?

Donna Andersen replies

OMG - he is a complete sociopath. Dump him immediately and never talk to him again.

Sociopaths say you're crazy – and you believe them

Lying and then lying to cover up the lies. Disappearing for days without explanation. Draining your finances. Cheating — and you have proof!

You are understandably upset. Justifiably angry.

Yet when you confront the perpetrator, not only does the sociopath deny, deny, deny, he or she says it never happened, you imagined it all, and you're paranoid. In fact, you're losing your mind! You should be committed!

You are so confused that you think the sociopath may be right. Are you losing your mind?

How does this happen? How does the sociopath lie, manipulate and deceive, yet you feel like you're the one going crazy?

The root of the problem is that when this person came into your life, you didn't know about sociopaths. Therefore, you are vulnerable to the sociopath's plot.

So here's what happens.

Step 1: The sociopath convinces you that it's love!

You meet and the sociopath sweeps you off your feet in a whirlwind romance. Or, you meet and don't like the sociopath, but he or she is so persistent that you finally decide to give the person a chance.

Either way, you interpret the sociopath's behavior to mean that he or she is smitten with you. Because who would be so attentive, or keep trying to see you, if they weren't head over heels crazy for you?

It must be love!

According to your understanding of life, people who are in love are kind to each other. They want the best for their partners and never intentionally hurt their beloved.

Since the sociopath is proclaiming undying love, that's what you expect.

Step 2: The sociopath lies about almost everything, but you don't know it

You don't realize that the caring behavior is a charade, and that all the sweet nothings that come out of his or her mouth are just that — nothing.

In fact, you don't realize that just about everything the sociopath says is a lie.

After all, the sociopath looks deep into your eyes, convincing you of his or her sincerity.

You know that some of what you're told is true. But you don't know that sociopaths are experts at mixing enough truth with their lies so that the entire story sounds like the truth.

Yes, sometimes the story doesn't make sense at first. But the sociopath explains away the discrepancies, and the explanations are always so plausible.

And then there are the times that the story is totally outrageous. But it has to be true, because no one would ever make up such a tale.

You certainly would never say such things if they weren't true, and you can't imagine that anyone would. Who would have the nerve to make those claims if the events hadn't really happened?

Sociopaths will do it — but you don't know that.

Step 3: The sociopath intentionally makes you doubt your perceptions

The sociopath's objective is power and control over you. That means the sociopath wants to control your mind.

One way to do that is to make you doubt your perceptions. It's called "gaslighting."

Sociopaths say you're crazy — and you believe them

According to Wikipedia:

> Gaslighting or gas-lighting is a form of mental abuse in which information is twisted or spun, selectively omitted to favor the abuser, or false information is presented with the intent of making victims doubt their own memory, perception, and sanity. Instances may range simply from the denial by an abuser that previous abusive incidents ever occurred, up to the staging of bizarre events by the abuser with the intention of disorienting the victim.

The term comes from the 1944 film, *Gaslight*, starring Ingrid Bergman as Paula.

In the movie, the sociopathic villain intentionally hides things, and then says Paula took or moved them. He has a violent outburst and then denies that it happened, saying Paula imagined it. He keeps this up through the entire movie, until Paula thinks she is insane.

Sociopaths actually do this.

One Lovefraud reader recounted how the sociopath kept moving her keys, and then criticized her for losing them. As another example, many sociopaths make promises, and then blatantly deny that the words were spoken. They are adamant. Vociferous. Indignant.

You would never intentionally move things just to confuse people. You might break a promise, but you would never deny that you made it.

So you wonder — did you really lose the keys again? Did you imagine what was said?

Step 4: The sociopath insists that you have mental problems

The sociopath proclaims true love, lies fluently without you realizing it, and then intentionally tries to make you doubt your perceptions.

While the sociopath lies and denies, he or she continually professes love for you.

In your mind, and in your way of life, love is about being caring and supportive. It's about trust. You would never dream of blatantly lying to someone you love, or intentionally treating them badly.

So you must have misunderstood. You must have imagined it. The only rational explanation is that you are losing your mind.

That's what the sociopath tells you. Consistently. Repeatedly.

"That never happened. You imagined it."

"Why are you so paranoid? You should go to counseling."

"I'm really getting concerned about you. You seem to be losing your grip on reality."

Learning the real truth

Eventually, somehow, you learn the truth: The sociopath has been lying all along. About everything.

This truth is devastating. Earth-shattering.

You didn't know that there were human beings who look and seem normal, but who have no heart, no conscience and no remorse.

Before you knew about sociopaths, you may have had a tendency to see people as you are, and interpret the actions of others in terms of how you would behave.

You had no idea that there are humans living among us who operate under a totally different set of rules. Or, make that no rules.

Once you learn about sociopaths, you realize that your perceptions were correct all along. Contrary to what the sociopath so forcefully stated, you are not crazy.

11 abusive behaviors you're likely to see from a sociopathic partner

When Lovefraud readers ask me for personal consultations, it's because someone in their lives — usually a romantic partner — acts in ways that they simply cannot understand. The readers describe an unfathomable mixture of affection, attention, contradictions, deception, blaming and rage. It makes no sense and it's behavior that they've never seen before.

So imagine the readers' surprise when I say, "Yeah, they all do that."

It's true. Sociopaths all seem to engage in the same abusive behaviors. Recognizing physical and sexual abuse is straightforward enough. You may also be aware of psychological and emotional abuse.

But if you're involved with a sociopath, you may also see some of the following:

1. Blaming you for his or her bad behavior

No matter what the sociopath does, from disappearing without explanation to cheating on you to physically assaulting you, he or she will say it's your fault. You weren't attentive enough, or you complained too much, or you pushed his or her buttons. They will tell you this with so much outrage that you may actually start to believe it.

2. The smear campaign

Long before you have any inkling that there is a problem in

your relationship, the sociopath is trashing you behind your back to family, friends, neighbors and the authorities. He or she may say that you're mentally ill, cheating, doing drugs, or other lies. The objective is to take down your support network, so that when you finally realize what is going on and reach out for help, no one believes you.

3. Telling you that no one else will want you

In the beginning of your involvement, the sociopath showered you with compliments — you were beautiful, smart, fun and sexy. Now, the sociopath tells you that you're old, fat, ugly and stupid. The sociopath says he or she stays with you out of obligation or pity, and you'll never find another partner. This is designed to weaken your confidence and self-esteem so that you are afraid to leave.

4. Constant calls and text messages

Early in your relationship the sociopath may have called and texted constantly, claiming he or she was head-over-heels for you. You may have though it was cute, proof of true love. But gradually the calls and texts became intrusive and are now used to control you. If you don't answer the call or text back immediately, he or she may fly into a rage.

5. Demanding to know everything you do

Calls and text messages are the first stage of controlling behavior. Eventually the sociopath may make you account for every minute of your day, demanding to know what you did, whom you spoke to and what was said. The consequences of providing the wrong answer: rage. Eventually you may be afraid to do anything without the sociopath's permission.

6. Relaying what others are supposedly saying about you

The sociopath may tell you that your family, friends and neighbors have bad opinions about you, or think there is something wrong with you. Everything the sociopath says is likely a lie, and he or she is fabricating all the stories, but you don't know that. The objective is to drive a wedge between you and your support network, so that you feel you can't turn to anyone for help.

7. Manipulating the money

Sociopaths typically drain you financially in one of two ways. 1) They get you to pay all the expenses and run up your credit cards until you are broke. 2) They convince you to quit your job, perhaps to take care of the kids, and make you financially dependent on them. Either way, when you've had enough and want to escape the relationship, you don't have the resources to leave.

8. Accusing you of cheating

Many sociopaths will accuse you of cheating on them. Even though they have no basis for making these accusations, they say you're sleeping with your co-workers or still involved with previous romantic interests. Why do they do this? Because they are cheating, so they assume you are also.

9. Using your deepest secrets against you

Back when you were in the honeymoon phase of your relationship — when the sociopath was showering you with attention and you thought it was true love — you may have shared some deeply personal information. Perhaps you'd once been abused. Or you had an addiction. Whatever. Eventually, the sociopath uses that personal information as ammunition to hurt you.

10. Electronic surveillance

Today's technology is great — but unfortunately it has a dark side. Software to monitor your computer and cell phone, GPS tracking devices, and tiny microphones to bug your home, are all cheap and easy to install. If you feel like the sociopath is reading your mind, it may actually be that he or she has you under surveillance.

11. Threatening suicide

As shocking as it may seem, threatening suicide is a typical sociopathic behavior. The idea is to guilt you into staying in the relationship. The sociopath may be bluffing with the suicide threats, or may be serious. Either way, know that you are not responsible. The best thing you can do is call 911.

Strategies of power and control

What you need to know about all of these behaviors is that they are sociopathic strategies of power and control. The sociopath does not engage in these behaviors just because of you. All of these forms of abuse come right out of the sociopath's playbook. He or she likely treated other people exactly the same way.

Why is it important to understand this? Because by recognizing that sociopaths engage in these behaviors all the time, you can take back your power. The sociopath's actions are not your fault. In fact, it doesn't matter what you do — the sociopath's behavior will not change.

So you might as well get out.

6 really bad reasons for staying with the sociopath

If you're reading Lovefraud, it's probably because you suspect that someone in your life is a sociopath.

This person's behavior has baffled you — how can he lie so prolifically? How can she be so cold? How can anyone behave so horribly and then act as if nothing happened?

So you went looking on the Internet for answers. You've plugged this person's upsetting behavior into your favorite search engine and come across a list of traits such as Lovefraud's Key Symptoms of a Sociopath. Check, check, check — the person exhibits all or most of them.

So what do you do now?

The correct answer is to get the person out of your life as quickly as possible.

But some people don't do that. Some people stay involved with the disordered individual. Here are reasons why — and why they're bad ideas.

I'll get him (or her) to therapy

On Lovefraud, sociopathy is a general term for the Cluster B personality disorders — antisocial, narcissistic, borderline, histrionic. These disorders define the way the person interacts with the world; they are ingrained into his or her identity.

Maybe treatment will be available in the future, but for now, once a sociopath is an adult, there is no rehabilitation. No drug or no therapy program has been proven to make any difference. In fact, there is research indicating that therapy makes sociopaths worse.

I love this person, and love conquers all

It doesn't matter how much you love, the sociopath is incapable of feeling love, and incapable of truly receiving your love. That is the core of the disorder — an inability to love.

But what about all the declarations of love this person spoke to you? It was playacting. Sociopaths say, "I love you," because they know that if they speak those words, they get what they want. The sweet nothings really are nothing.

I can outsmart the sociopath

You very well may be smarter than the sociopath, but it's unlikely that you can beat a sociopath at his or her own game.

The sociopath has no conscience and no remorse. This means the sociopath has no qualms about engaging in vicious, underhanded lies and attacks. The sociopath's objective is to win, and he or she will play dirty — very, very dirty — in order to achieve that objective.

The kids need their father (or mother)

If the father or mother is a sociopath — no, they don't need this person. Remember, sociopaths are incapable of feeling love, and that includes love for their own children. Sociopaths are terrible parents. At the very least, they are disinterested. At worst, they are highly abusive, or they actively teach the kids to engage antisocial behavior.

If you can manage it, the best thing to do is get the sociopathic parent out of your life, and your kids' lives as well. Sometimes, unfortunately, the sociopath won't let this happen. In this case, do your best to keep contact to a minimum.

I want my money back

The sociopath has drained your finances and put you into debt. He or she may have convinced you to invest everything you have into some sure-to-succeed business deal — except the deal

6 really bad reasons for staying with the sociopath

failed. He or she is promising to pay everything back. It's very possible that the sociopath has no intention of keeping that promise.

If the sociopath has no job, no money, no credit and no assets — well, any money you gave him or her could be gone. You may have to just write off your losses and move on.

I know there's good inside

No, there isn't. All your life, you've heard cultural messages like "we're all created equal" and "deep down, we're all the same" — well, these bromides do not apply to everyone.

Sociopaths are empty suits, cardboard cut-outs, automatons — use whatever term helps you understand that there really is nothing inside.

So, if you realize that there's a sociopath in your life, but you're considering staying involved with this person for some of the above reasons, know that the longer you stay, the harder it's going to be to get out. Please change your mind and leave as quickly as possible.

4 reasons why psychopaths will never stop cheating

Do you have absolute proof that your partner is cheating — but he or she denies it?

When you confront your partner about cheating, does he or she say it's your fault?

Does your partner pick a fight with you, and use the fight as an excuse to storm out of the house and see someone else?

If you answer yes to these questions, you may be involved with a psychopath — for more warning signs, get the exclusive Lovefraud checklist.

If your partner checks a lot of the boxes on the checklist, know this: There's nothing you can do, or could have ever done, to prevent or stop the cheating — no matter what your partner says.

Here are four reasons why psychopaths will never stop cheating.

1. All psychopaths want in life are power, control and sex

Psychopaths are wired differently from the rest of us. If you're a relatively normal person, you want love in your life. You cherish your important relationships. You want to feel connected to other people.

Psychopaths don't. They view other people as objects to be manipulated.

Psychopaths are incapable of feeling love, so it means nothing to them. Instead, they derive their satisfaction from power, control and sex.

4 reasons why psychopaths will never stop cheating

2. For psychopaths, romantic relationships are the means to an end

Here's what happens when psychopaths meet you:

- They evaluate you to see if you have anything that they want.
- They figure out your vulnerabilities
- They manipulate your vulnerabilities to get what they want.

Psychopaths look at a romantic partner as someone to supply them with sex, a home, money, an image of respectability — whatever.

They are always looking for new sources of supply, so if they encounter someone who may have something else that they want — well, they just go through the above steps with the new target.

3. Psychopaths view romantic relationships as entertainment

As stated above, psychopaths pursue romantic relationships because they want something. Sometimes, what they want is simply entertainment.

They like being the puppet master — pulling strings to get you to respond. They experience "duping delight" — they get a charge out of pulling one over on you.

So sometimes, they pursue you just to see if they can hook you. When they succeed, game over, and they dump you with no consideration at all for your feelings.

4. Psychopaths are always looking for a new sexual thrill

Psychopaths have a need for excitement — including sexual excitement. Because they get bored easily, they're always on the lookout for a new type of sex.

This could mean a new sexual partner. Or, it could mean a new experience — same-sex encounters, pedophilia, bondage, sado-masochism.

You may feel like a psychopath's interest in sex has waned. It may not be their interest in sex — just sex with you. They're still looking for someone or something new and exciting.

Setting yourself free

Here is the benefit of knowing that your partner is disordered: The knowledge gives you the power to set yourself free.

Despite what the psychopaths say, their behavior is not your fault, and it never was. They are going to cheat, and there is nothing you can do about it.

So do not blame yourself. Do not feel guilty. Don't feel like you need to honor your commitment to him or her — it was never a mutual commitment.

Give yourself permission to leave, recover and find the loving partner that you truly deserve.

Why falling for a romance scam doesn't mean you're stupid

A woman from Queensland, Australia, trying to help her online lover, found herself in the middle of a $6 million romance scam.

The 60-year-old woman met the man, who claimed to be American, 18 months earlier. He convinced her to send him $100,000 of her own money. Then she gave the man her bank details, and he deposited $6 million into her account — money that had been swindled from a South Korean business.

In a news article on ABC.net.au, a detective sergeant gave his opinion of the woman's actions in the romance scam: "I think it's just blatant stupidity — there's no other word for it."

Those of us who've lost money to sociopathic love interests usually do feel stupid, once we learn that we've been scammed. But are we?

Another scam — leading to tragedy

In another case from Australia, someone stole the identity of Lincoln Lewis, a heartthrob TV actor, and began an online relationship with a young woman called "Emma." It all seemed believable to Emma, because she actually knew Lincoln Lewis — they had gone to primary school together, and she had dated one of his best friends. But the entire relationship was a lie.

This type of romance scam is called catfishing — using online aliases to lure someone into a relationship. I encourage you to read the story — *Catching a catfish: A terrifying story of virtual* deceit and inexplicable malice, perpetrated by the last person anyone expected,* on ABC.net.au. The twists and turns are unbelievable. The catfisher was ultimately caught — but not before causing terrible tragedy to the victims.

It's not stupidity — it's humanity

But back to the "stupid" comment. In a follow-up article on the same website, an online fraud expert, Suli Malet-Warden, said that the victims aren't falling for the romance scams because of stupidity. Rather, they are reacting to the complex language of love. Scammers shower their targets with validating messages. She said victims are:

> "Being told how much they are loved, how wonderful they are ... they use that sort of validating language and the prolific nature of it, regular text messages not just through the day, but through the night.
>
> "The victim is then expecting those validating messages to come through. They're incredibly supportive, they're appealing, they're flattering, they're soothing."

This language, Malet-Warden explains, causes the victim's brain to release chemicals related to falling in love — adrenaline, norepinephrine and oxytocin. Oxytocin causes the target to feel trust for the scammer. Plus, the scammer isolates the target from family and friends, eliminating potential reality checks. The target doesn't stand a chance.

So it's not stupidity that makes us fall for romance scams. It's our humanity.

Following are totally normal aspects of human social interaction that sociopaths hijack in order to take advantage of us.

Oxytocin — the cuddle chemical

Oxytocin, a neurotransmitter and hormone, plays a huge role in bonding. Whenever we experience intimacy with a person — and intimacy can be anything from a conversation to a hug to sex — oxytocin is released into the bloodstream. It makes us trust the person with whom we experience intimacy.

When sociopaths pile on words of love and validation — whether communicating in person or online — they cause our bodies to flood us with oxytocin. The oxytocin makes us trust the sociopath. So when they start asking for money or anything else, we are primed to comply with what they want.

Most sociopaths probably don't know the biology of how this works. But they do know that if they can convince us to trust them, they get what they want.

Targeting our emotions

Sociopaths snag us by aiming right for our emotions. This makes sense, because the whole point of a romance is an emotional connection. According to *These are the 4 emotions scammers often prey on to trick us,* on IrishExaminer.com, they target our:

Desire. When we want something, we are vulnerable. Most people want to be loved, want a companion, want to feel valued. Sociopaths seem to offer us precisely what we desire. It's hard to say no.

Excitement. It's exciting to fall in love. If we've been waiting a long time for romance, it's thrilling to finally find it. Sociopaths ramp up the excitement with their over-the-top proclamations of love and promises for the future.

Trust. The human race survived and thrived because of our ability to trust. It's hardwired into our biology (see above). Sociopaths prey on it.

Fear of missing out. We don't want to feel doubts about a romantic partner, because that would mean giving up our dreams of togetherness. What if we're wrong? If we end the involvement, will we miss the great love of our life?

Taking advantage of social principles

Over millennia, societies have developed guidelines for social behavior that we've all internalized. Or at least, all of us who are socially normal have internalized them. Sociopaths are aware of the rules of social conduct, but bend or break them to get what they want.

Here are principles of social behavior that sociopaths take advantage of, according to TheConversation.com:

Principle of reciprocity. When someone does something for us, we feel obligated to do something for them. This is called "forced indebtedness." Sociopaths often help us, or give us something, precisely to make us indebted to them, so we later give them what they want.

Principle of similarity. Research shows that we tend to like people who seem to be the same as us, and we are more likely to agree with what they want. That's why sociopaths claim to have all the same likes and dislikes as we do. In fact, sometimes they present themselves to be our twin.

Little steps. We like to think of ourselves as consistent. When we say we are going to do something, most of us want to follow through. Sociopaths take advantage of this by asking us to do small, easy things at first — perhaps a small loan that they pay back. We get in the habit of saying yes, and then it becomes difficult to say no.

Raising awareness

In the end, we don't fall for sociopaths and romance scams because of stupidity. Sociopaths use our own human nature against us — our desire for connection, our need to trust, our willingness to be helpful.

But there is another part of our human nature that will protect us — our intuition.

Our intuition is designed to protect us from predators. So we'll usually feel an uneasiness, an internal nudge, that something about a person or situation is not right. But often we're afraid to cut someone out of our lives based on a "feeling." Being aware of how sociopaths manipulate our normal human nature will help us analyze what is going on. The key to protecting ourselves is noticing our instincts, and then acting on them.

Deception: the sociopath's key strategy

My blog article last week was entitled, *Why falling for a romance scam doesn't mean you're stupid*. I related several stories of people who thought they were in romantic relationships, but everything their so-called partners told them was a lie. One woman lost $100,000. Another lost her life.

In response to the article, I received the following comment from a reader:

> I've figured out that the common denominator with all these love scams, is lack of SELF love!
> Why are there so many ppl that don't love themselves enough to not place themselves in these crazy scenarios?

In some cases, there may be truth to this observation — yes, some people do not think highly of themselves. But I do not believe that a lack of self-love is the main reason why people end up in fake relationships with sociopaths.

Sociopath's strategy of deception

The key strategy that sociopaths use to seduce their unsuspecting targets is deception. They lie. They forge documentation. They create elaborate schemes of fake friends and family members who supposedly vouch for them.

The whole point of deception is that the target doesn't realize that he or she is being deceived.

For skilled liars like sociopaths, deception is easy. They've been doing it all their lives. But for the rest of us, spotting deception is hard. In fact, research shows that on average, people can spot a lie only 53% of the time. That's not much better than flipping a coin.

Add in the fact that the target wants to believe all of the flattery, compliments and promises of the sociopath — well, most people don't stand a chance.

My involvement with a sociopath

My ex-husband, James Montgomery, was a total fraud who scammed me for more than a quarter-million dollars. How did he do it? He deceived me.

He presented himself to be a war hero and a successful businessman. He talked like a war hero and successful businessman. He shared his military commendations — I didn't know that they were forged. He introduced me to his business partners. They'd been deceived as well.

Yes, I had some vulnerabilities — I was single and wanted a partner. But I was a successful, confident business owner. I had a lot of friends who cared about me. When James Montgomery came into my life, I felt like I'd finally met the man that I deserved.

I was not suffering from a lack of self-love. I was deceived.

Many other Lovefraud readers feel exactly the same way.

Protection through awareness

So what's the answer? How do we protect ourselves from romance scams?

The first step is awareness.

Sociopaths exist. They live all among us. They appear at first to be normal, but their motivations are totally different. Their goal is to exploit us.

When we know that sociopaths are out there, and we know that they lie, we have the fundamental tools to protect ourselves.

Why did I want to hug the sociopath, even though I know he is bad?

Lovefraud recently received the following email from a reader who posts as "amhealing2012."

>Miss Donna, I spoke by email to you about 2 years ago about a guy I had been dating. You confirmed he was indeed a sociopath.
>
>I have had no contact at all for over a year and a half. Strangely he has been on my mind a lot the last few weeks, thinking I saw him and thinking about him. Today while coming out of the mall with my older daughter I heard his voice say, "I hope you found what you were looking for." I turned and there he was with that cute grin on his face. IF not for my daughter being by me pushing me and saying, "mom just keep walking," I would have gone and hugged him.
>
>What the hell????? It was just like a magnet, drawing me to him!!! WHY??? After all this time and work on healing and no contact and reading and becoming wiser, WHY?
>
>I KNOW he IS toxic refuse! His sweet facade is FAKE and underneath is venom!!! So WHY the draw and magnet after all this time? HOW do I heal and get totally free of his, whatever it is?
>
>My daughter says it's cuz some people like to be abused. NO I don't think I do, I hate it, it hurts like hell

and took about a year to get past the GREAT pain of his abuse and betrayal of me. I even had to leave the church I had been at for 5 years; he poisoned most of the leadership towards me and stalked whatever service I chose to go to.

Anyhow, it's making me angry. I loved him and still do care about him, BUT know what he IS. Knowing that, WHY the magnet still? Am I not healed and not learned my lesson — or what the hay??

I will hush now, just a bit shocked at my reaction. He texted my phone even a bit later to say, "It was a nice surprise seeing you." ASS!! I almost answered saying I sensed I would see him. (As he has been heavily on my mind, as I said.)

I assumed it was the Lord warning me, but my reaction still surprised me. To be drawn to hug and warmly greet a freak??? Thank the Lord my daughter was with me.

After I found my brain and wondered what happened that I would even think of a warm anything towards him, my daughter yelled and told him to stay the f... away from me. I am sure that didn't help challenging him. :-(sigh. HELP please.

Thank you Miss Donna and thank you for this site. Not sure where I would be or have been without it.

— amhealing2012

P.S. – does this mean I am not healed or as far along as I thought I was????

Donna Andersen replies

Amhealing2012 —
Here's the good news: You were tested, and you passed.

Yes, you had a bit of help from your daughter — I'm very glad she was there with you, and able to support you in the critical moment. But even though you were shocked by your own initial reaction, you quickly recovered.

You have no doubt about what is best for you — continued No Contact.

You are not wondering if your assessment of him as toxic is

Why did I want to hug the sociopath, even though I know he is bad?

wrong, and maybe he's not so bad after all.

You are not hoping that he has changed, and you'll be able to reunite and live happily ever after.

You are firm in your resolve that he is a no-good etc., etc., etc. (I loved your emphatic and colorful description.)

So why did you feel an initial urge to hug him?

Psychological bond

Human beings are social creatures. We are supposed to bond. This is how the human race survived and evolved over millennia — by living together. The mechanism that enables us to live together over a long period of time is bonding.

The bond that develops with romantic partners is especially powerful, and it has several components.

One component is the psychological bond. Early in the involvement, when everything is fabulous, your new romance brings you pleasure. Pleasure sparks attachment, which is the beginning of the psychological bond. This is normal and natural.

When your romantic partner is a sociopath, however, a couple of things are different.

Most sociopaths, when they have targeted someone, engage in relentless love bombing. They shower you with attention. They want to be around you all the time. They make you feel like the most important person in the world.

As a result, the pleasure you feel is intensified, which makes for a stronger psychological bond.

Then, sociopaths do something to rock the romantic boat. Perhaps they suddenly disappear. Or you catch them flirting with someone else. Or they ask to borrow money and don't pay you back. You feel worry or doubt about the relationship, which causes fear and/or anxiety.

Surprisingly, this fear and anxiety actually makes the psychological bond stronger.

You want the relationship to go back to those heady days in the beginning. So you try to resolve the issue, which, of course, the sociopath probably fabricated. Perhaps you even apologize for something that you didn't do. Eventually you get back together, you feel relieved — and the psychological bond is strengthened again.

This becomes a continuing cycle of pleasure — fear and anxiety — relief. And with each turn of the wheel, the psychological bond you feel becomes stronger and stronger, until it is very difficult to break.

Your brain

In addition to the psychological aspects of bonding, there are also biological components.

We've written previously on Lovefraud about oxytocin. This is a hormone/neurotransmitter that causes us to feel calm, trusting and content, and alleviates fear and anxiety.

Oxytocin is released into our bloodstream and brain any time we experience intimacy — emotional sharing, physical touching, and especially sex. As a result, we trust the individual who caused the spike in oxytocin.

Plus, when we have sex with someone, it causes structural changes in our brains, making this person important to us. Again, this is all normal. Mother Nature set this up to encourage parents to stay together to raise children, so that the human race could survive.

The point is that when you develop a love bond with someone, it is strong, deep and hooked into your brain.

At least that's how YOU feel. Sociopaths do not bond the way the rest of us do. This is one reason why they are able to dump us and move on without looking back.

So Amhealing2012, when you suddenly and unexpectedly ran into the sociopath, it probably activated the remnants of the psychological and biological bond you once felt. Which is why you wanted to hug him.

More healing

You also asked if you are not yet healed. You have certainly made tremendous progress on your healing journey. But perhaps you do have a bit of mopping up to do.

You shouldn't look at this encounter as a failure. You should

Why did I want to hug the sociopath, even though I know he is bad?

look at it as an opportunity to clear out the last remaining remnants of the hold that this man once had on you.

You might also reflect on why this man was on your mind before you ran into him. You said you kept thinking about him — what were your thoughts? Where they positive or negative thoughts?

There are people who believe that we attract what we think about — and that's why it's important to use our willpower to control our thoughts.

Or, this might have been a lesson in listening to your intuition. Perhaps God or your intuition (which I think are highly related) was warning you that the guy was going to cross your path, so that you could be ready.

In any event, you did fine. Your initial impulse shocked you, but you did not act on that impulse. You put your emotional and psychological health first and stayed away from him.

I'm willing to bet that if you ever run into this man again, you'll have no desire to hug him.

5 reasons why we fall for con artists

We discover that our romantic partner is a complete and utter fake.

The proclamations of love, the stories of his or her past — nothing was true. All the money that our partner desperately needed — or promised would buy a life of luxury for the two of us — well, that evaporated into expensive and unnecessary toys, or a secret life with one or more other lovers (targets).

When it finally sinks in that we've been conned, the first question we ask of ourselves is, "How could I have been so stupid?"

Followed by, "Why didn't I see this coming?"

Feeling like chumps, we come down really hard on ourselves. But we aren't the only ones who are blind to the social predators living among us — our entire society is blind.

The fact that millions of sociopaths live among us is like a giant skeleton in the closet of the human race that nobody wants to talk about. This sets us up to be victimized.

Sociopathic con artists take advantage of this collective and individual blindness. With the skill that comes from practicing their craft from a very young age, they manipulate our empathy and emotions. They use us to accomplish their objectives du jour, whatever they may be.

So here's why we end up in romantic relationships with sociopathic con artists:

Reason #1 - We don't know sociopaths exist

Most people think sociopaths are all criminals and deranged

serial killers — this isn't necessarily true. Social predators live among us, and most of them never kill anyone. Still, these people have no heart, no conscience and no remorse.

The numbers are staggering. Lovefraud uses the term "sociopath" to cover all social predators — people who would be clinically diagnosed as being antisocial, psychopathic, narcissistic, borderline or histrionic. If you add up the official estimates of people with these conditions, perhaps 12% to 16% of the population — 30 million adults in the US — have personality disorders that make them unsuitable to be romantic partners.

And we, as a society, don't know it.

Reason #2 - We believe people are basically the same

In the United States, from the time we are small children, we are bombarded with messages about fairness, equal opportunity, giving people a chance and tolerance. In school, we learn that we're all created equal. In church, we learn that we're all God's children.

As a result, we believe all people are basically the same, there is good in everyone, and everyone just wants to be loved. Unfortunately, there is a segment of the population for which this simply is not true.

Sociopaths view the world as predators and prey — they are the predators, and everyone else is prey. They are not motivated by love; they are motivated by power and control. These people pursue romantic relationships not for love, but for exploitation.

Reason #3 — Humans are lousy lie detectors

Research shows that people can identify a lie only 53% of the time — not much better than flipping a coin.

All those signs that are supposedly giveaways that someone is lying — like looking away, failing to make eye contact — well, they simply don't apply when a sociopath is doing the lying.

Sociopaths are expert liars. They spend their whole lives lying. They feel entitled to lie. They lie for the fun of it. In fact, there's a phenomenon called "duping delight" — sociopaths get a thrill out of staring right into their targets' eyes and pulling the wool over them.

People who are not liars never see it coming.

Reason #4 — Sociopaths hijack the normal human bonding process

Trust is the glue that holds society together. Trust is so important to the human race that it is programmed into our biology.

A hormone called oxytocin is released in our brain and bloodstream whenever we feel intimacy — emotional or physical. Oxytocin then makes us feel calm, trusting and content, and alleviates fear and anxiety. Nature created this process to make people want to stay together to raise children.

When sociopaths target us for romantic relationships, they either spend a lot of time building what seems to be trust, or they rush us into emotional, physical or sexual intimacy. Either way, they get the oxytocin flowing in our brains, which makes us trust them. They keep piling on the intimacy, and we, to our detriment, keep trusting.

Reason #5 — The betrayal bond makes it difficult to escape

Once the love bond is in place, the sociopath does things that create fear and anxiety in us — like cheating on us, or taking more and more money.

Contrary to what we might expect, instead of driving us away, this actually makes the bond we feel with the sociopath stronger. It becomes a betrayal bond — a powerful bond that we feel with someone who is destructive to us.

We want desperately to return to the heady experience of the beginning of our involvement, which was filled with what we believed was love and affection. We keep waiting for the sociopath to make the situation right.

But he or she never does. The exploitation continues.

Betrayal bonds are highly addictive and difficult to break. That's why we stay in the relationship far longer than we should — until we can no longer escape the fact that we've been conned.

Seriously lacking: 'Savvy Senior' advice about online dating

Savvy Senior, a syndicated column that appears in more than 400 newspapers and magazines across the United States, calls itself an information service for baby boomers and senior citizens. The author, Jim Miller, published an article called *Looking for love and companionship online.* It started with a question from a reader:

> Dear Savvy Senior: What can you tell me about online dating for older people? My daughter has been urging me to give it a try, but at age 62, I'm a little hesitant. Lonely Senior

Miller responded by describing the mechanics of online dating—how to choose a dating site and how to create a profile. He encouraged seniors to "make an effort" and not get discouraged. He did include the obligatory cautions: Be prudent about giving out your full name, address and phone number. The first meeting should be in a public place. For extra caution, spend a few dollars on a quick background check. He also noted that some people will exaggerate or flat-out lie in their profiles.

The overall theme was that "dating websites are an easy way to meet hundreds of new single people without ever having to leave your home." In my opinion, Miller's words of caution were nowhere near emphatic enough.

Meeting predators online

In 2011, as part of my research for *Red Flags of Love Fraud,*

I conducted the Lovefraud Romantic Partner Survey. Ten percent of the respondents—131 people, mostly women—were age 51 or older when a sociopath came into their life. This is the age group that the Savvy Senior writes about.

Here's the scary part: 39% of the survey's 51-and-over respondents met the sociopath on the Internet. By comparison, only 21% of respondents aged 50 and under met the sociopath on the Internet. So the proportion of baby boomers and senior citizens who met sociopaths online was almost double that of the younger survey respondents.

Anyone who engages in online dating needs to clearly understand the risks. The basics are spelled out in the Lovefraud post, *Dangers of online dating*. I am reproducing that article below.

Dangers of online dating

1. Worldwide, there are 1.8 billion Internet users. It is reasonable to assume that, as in the general population, 1% to 4% of them have antisocial personality disorder. That means there between 14 million and 72 million antisocials online—all trolling for victims.
2. Sociopaths target lonely people. If you're looking for a relationship online, you are advertising the fact that you're lonely. You are setting yourself up to be exploited.
3. When filling out an online dating profile, you provide information about yourself and what you are looking for. Sociopaths take the information and pretend to be the person of your dreams. They use the information that you posted to seduce you.
4. Sociopaths typically register on multiple dating sites simultaneously. They keep baiting the hook until someone bites.

Seriously lacking: 'Savvy Senior' advice about online dating

5. The Internet is anonymous. It is impossible to know for sure with whom you are corresponding. Some people post gorgeous photos in their profiles, which are actually photos of models stolen from elsewhere on the Internet.
6. Experts believe that 65% to 90% of human communication is nonverbal—facial expressions, gestures, body language, tone of voice. That means in communication via the web or email, 65% to 90% of the meaning is missing. With so much information missing, you interpret a communication to mean what you want it to mean.
7. Because communicating over the Internet is anonymous, it creates a sense of safety. You feel like you can confess your hopes and dreams to a stranger.
8. Sociopaths say what their targets want to hear. Often, the sociopaths are lying. But humans can detect a lie only 53% of the time— about the same as flipping a coin.
9. So here's what happens when you look for romance online:
    - You provide information about yourself by filling out the dating profile.
    - You communicate with someone, but 65% to 90% of the meaning is missing.
    - You pour out your heart and soul, and it feels good.
    - The person responds, and you interpret everything to mean what you want it to mean.
    - You fall in love with your own fantasy.

More cautions for baby boomers and seniors

Besides those nine points, boomers and seniors who consider online dating need to know the following:

First, if you are divorced and your marriage was bad, you are vulnerable. Unless you have actively worked on recovery, you're probably still carrying the pain of previous abuse, emptiness or betrayal. You may feel desperate to find a fulfilling relationship, which makes you susceptible to sociopathic love bombing.

Second, if you are widowed and your marriage was good, you are vulnerable. Having enjoyed a loving, supportive partnership, you may believe that all relationships are that way. This may make you unwilling to believe that a new partner's motives may be exploitative.

Finally, describing your status as "widowed" in a dating profile sets you up to be exploited. Sociopaths know you may have assets, a life insurance payout, a home that is now yours alone. They know you are bereaved. You are a fat target waiting to be plucked.

Sociopaths continue their exploitative ways all their lives. My ex-husband was still trying to seduce women online as he approached age 70. Several Lovefraud readers have told me stories of their lonely fathers who were seduced by gray-haired grannies who were looking for a meal ticket.

Yes, sometimes online dating works — my own widowed sister-in-law found love on a dating site. But everyone needs to understand the risks, and the warning signs that a new beau is actually an exploiter.

The Lonely Senior who wrote to Savvy Senior is right to be hesitant.

To the psychopath, the relationship meant nothing

One of the hardest parts of ending a romantic involvement with a psychopath is accepting that to him or her, the relationship never meant anything.

In the beginning, when the psychopath pursued you, showered you with attention and affection, called and texted all day long — it was just seduction.

When the psychopath proclaimed undying love, declared that you were the best thing to ever happen to him or her, pushed the relationship along while painting a glistening image of the future — it was all to hook you before you escaped.

When the rough patches came and you were ready to walk away, and the psychopath pleaded, cajoled, promised to change, or even threatened to commit suicide if you left — it was all to maintain control over you. The psychopath wasn't finished with you yet.

Then, when you finally decided there would be no more chances, the relationship was completely and irreparably over, and the psychopath went after the money, property and kids with a vengeance — well, that's because the psychopath's only real goals in life are power, control and winning.

Profoundly different

So how do you deal with this? How do you accept that all the professions of love were lies, and all the promises were worthless?

What's necessary is to come to terms with the fact that psychopaths are fundamentally and profoundly different from the rest of us.

They are empty suits. Aliens. Cardboard cut-outs. Use whatever analogy helps you understand that psychopaths are missing the traits and qualities that make the rest of us human.

They do not feel remorse, guilt or shame. If they appear to show these emotions, they are acting.

They do not have the ability to love. They do not truly care about anyone else's happiness and well-being. If they do things that seem to be supportive, it's because the actions further their agenda.

You will never be able to understand how they think and why they do what they do. You just need to accept that they are what they are.

What was real?

By this point, you're probably wondering, what was real?

YOU were real. Your love, caring and trust were authentic. You did your part, in fact, you did far more than your part, no matter what the psychopath says.

You opened your heart, which is something the psychopath never did, and is incapable of doing. Unfortunately, you were deceived by someone who took advantage of your good nature and your love.

You have a heart. The psychopath does not.

To Mom and Dad: 9 reasons why your son or daughter fell for the sociopath

Dear Parents of a Lovefraud Target,

Your son or daughter has now come to the brutal realization that the entire relationship was a scam.

Perhaps you've had your suspicions for a while. Perhaps you've even tried to tell your kid that the partner was no good, but he or she wouldn't listen to you.

Now everything has collapsed, and you can't understand why your son or daughter didn't see it coming.

Please understand that sociopaths are professional con artists, and they are really, really good at what they do. In fact, they spend their entire lives perfecting their craft.

Following are nine reasons why your son or daughter fell for it.

1. Your son or daughter didn't know sociopaths exist

Our society tells us that everyone is created equal, everyone just wants to be loved, and there's good in everyone. Perhaps you even said these things to your child. If not, the messages certainly came through at school.

Our society doesn't tell us that there are exceptions. The feel-good characterizations simply do not apply to the approximately 12% of women and 16% of men who are personality disordered.

These exploiters come from all demographic groups and all walks of life. They are not necessarily hard-core drug addicts or criminals.

What we all need to learn is that people who are attractive, educated and well-mannered can also be evil.

2. Your son or daughter is good and kind-hearted

Perhaps you taught your children to treat others the way they want to be treated. Your son or daughter may be naturally kind and willing to help others.

Usually, this is a wonderful way to live. Unfortunately, there are people in the world — sociopaths — who are willing to take advantage of anyone's goodness, kindness and generosity.

We all tend to interpret the way others behave according to the way we behave. So if we don't lie, and would never dream of intentionally hurting someone, we don't know it's possible for another person to do it to us.

That makes us walking targets for sociopaths.

3. Sociopaths are extremely convincing liars

It is impossible to overstate a sociopath's ability to lie. These people lie like they breathe. They spend their entire lives perfecting their lies. They tell big lies and small lies. They tell outrageous lies. They even lie when they'd be better off telling the truth.

Sociopaths can look deep into your eyes and lie. All of those tips about how to spot a liar simply do not work with sociopaths. These people can pass lie detector tests.

If your son or daughter is basically honest, they never stood a chance.

4. Sociopaths promise to make dreams come true

In the beginning of the involvement, the sociopath likely asked your son or daughter a lot of questions, and listened very carefully to their answers. Your kid likely interpreted this to mean that the sociopath was really, totally interested in them.

Actually, the sociopath was listening carefully to find out your child's hopes and dreams. The sociopath wanted to discover the deepest place within them to set the seduction hook — by promising to make the dreams come true.

And who doesn't want to believe someone who promises to make your dreams come true?

5. Sociopaths target vulnerabilities

If we're human, we have vulnerabilities. Sociopaths are experts at finding and exploiting them.

This doesn't necessarily mean that your son or daughter lacks intelligence, has low self-esteem, or is a co-dependent personality. We all have desires, and what we want makes us vulnerable. We also all have emotional wounds, and those wounds make us vulnerable.

Many times emotional wounds date back to childhood. Can you think of anything your son or daughter experienced that could have created a wound?

6. Sociopaths hijack the natural human bonding process

When people experience intimacy, a hormone called oxytocin is released into the bloodstream and brain. Oxytocin is triggered by any type of intimacy — emotional sharing, physical touching and sex. Oxytocin makes us trust the person with whom we share intimacy.

Feelings of love cause dopamine to be released in the brain. Dopamine is associated with energy, motivation and addiction.

These psychological and biological changes are normal. Nature intended them to make us want to stay with our romantic partners to care for children.

But none of them apply to sociopaths. These disordered people do not form normal psychological bonds. But they intentionally do things — like causing fear and anxiety — that make it difficult for their partners to break the psychological bonds and escape.

7. Sociopaths present themselves as perfect partners

In the beginning, it seems like the sociopath has so much in common with your son or daughter. That's because sociopaths figure out what their targets are looking for, and then make themselves into that person.

Then, sociopaths keep the mask on as long as necessary to get the target hooked. Once the target is committed — perhaps living together, married or pregnant — the sociopath may totally change.

I've heard of sociopaths who even announced immediately after the wedding, "Now I can stop pretending."

8. Sociopaths engage in brainwashing

Cult leaders — who are sociopaths in the extreme — have discovered that the most effective brainwashing technique is love bombing. This means is showering their targets with attention and affection, making the target feel loved and wanted.

The sociopath your son or daughter encountered likely did this in the beginning of the relationship. That's how they got hooked.

From there, the sociopath may have gradually engaged in mind control by manipulating your kid's behavior, information, thoughts and emotions. The sociopath likely instilled an "us vs. them" mentality in your son or daughter, with you being the bad guys. This is a typical thought control tactic.

Sociopaths instinctively know to do this. But their targets, unfortunately, are not aware of what is happening.

9. A premeditated scam

Everything the sociopath did to take advantage of your son or daughter was intentional.

Here's what sociopaths do when they meet a potential target:

- Evaluate the target to see if he or she has anything that they want.
- Ask questions to determine the target's vulnerabilities.
- Use the target's vulnerabilities to take what they want.

The entire relationship was a scam. The sociopath may have been a "make it up as you go along" type of person. Or, the sociopath may have executed a plan that was years in the making. (Yes, that happens.)

This is mind-boggling. No one wants to believe that promises of love and devotion are just a ruse. So even if your son or daughter started having doubts, they never even dreamed of the scope of the sociopath's betrayal.

What to do now

Please understand that your son or daughter was up against a professional. The sociopath targeted your kid, and used love bombing, lies, mind control, emotional manipulation, fear and guilt to execute the exploitation scheme.

The sociopath probably did not employ all those tactics with you. Therefore, you may have been able to see what was going on, where your son or daughter could not.

Mom and Dad, if your kid now knows they've been scammed, the pain of betrayal is overwhelming. The last thing they need to hear from you is, "I told you so."

The best thing you can do is focus on your love for your brokenhearted child, and without judgment, help him or her pick up the pieces.

Psychopathy can run in families — a possible warning for you

Lovefraud recently received the following request in an email from a reader:

> My husband's psychopathy was never diagnosed as far as I know, but some years after we married, and her second suicide attempt that I knew of, he told me his mother had been diagnosed as a psychopathic manic depressive.
>
> Maybe you could give your readers 'a heads up and how to' on finding out as much as possible about the in-laws' medical conditions before marriage, better yet, sound them out before becoming emotionally entangled?

This is a great suggestion, so thank you to this Lovefraud reader.

Here's my basic advice: Understand that psychopathy can run in families. So if you see or hear about bad or disturbing behavior by relatives of your romantic partner, pay attention.

Highly genetic

Psychopathy is highly genetic. What that means is that a person can be born with a predisposition, a genetic risk, to develop a psychopathic personality disorder.

There is, however, an interaction between nature and nurture. Whether a child with genetic risk actually develops the disorder may depend on the type of parenting that he or she receives, or other factors in the child's environment.

Research has shown that harsh and inconsistent parenting is associated with a child developing callous and unemotional traits, which can be precursors to psychopathy.

Usually, if a child is genetically at risk, it's because one or both of the parents has psychopathic traits. Psychopaths are notoriously bad parents. So the child gets not only bad genes, but bad parenting as well.

It's a recipe for producing another psychopath. And it can happen over and over again in some families.

The psychopathic seduction

In the initial love-bombing phase of the relationship, psychopaths can shower you with attention and affection. This person seems to be your perfect mate, the one you've been waiting for all your life.

But if the person is actually disordered, the caring behavior is all a charade.

Some psychopaths are capable of keeping the charade going for a long time — years, even — as long as you are useful to them. Although you may sense that something is not right, you may not be able to pinpoint that the person is engaging in manipulation and deceit. You may doubt yourself, because your partner seems to want you so much.

The psychopath is engaging in impression management. But what about his or her family members?

Warning signs among the relatives

If you hear about any of the following regarding your partner's blood relatives, pay attention:

1. Criminal behavior
2. Abusive behavior
3. Domestic violence
4. Any kind of violence

5. Diagnosis of antisocial or narcissistic personality disorder, or psychopathy
6. Multiple short-term romantic partners
7. Scams or other financial crimes
8. Drug or alcohol addictions
9. Child molestation
10. Prison sentences

Of course, it is very possible for a person with a normal ability to love and a conscience to be born into a family that has psychopaths. In fact, many Lovefraud readers, who are themselves empathetic, have realized that one or both of their parents are psychopaths.

But as the saying goes, "The apple doesn't fall far from the tree."

If your partner's relatives exhibit the traits or behaviors listed above, it may mean that your partner is also capable of the behavior, once the psychopathic mask slips.

Problem children

If your partner has kids, you should also pay close attention to how he or she treats them, and the behavior of the children.

If you see flashes of harsh, inconsistent or other types of bad parenting, they may be indications of your partner's true nature, and not just that the kids were acting up that day.

And if the children are deceitful, manipulative or aggressive, well, those traits came from somewhere, either your partner's family or the ex's family.

Meeting the family

Some families of psychopathic individuals will tell you about their disturbing behavior — but some won't.

The family may actually be clueless about the true nature of his or her personality, especially if they live far away.

Or, even worse, the family may know about antisocial or abusive behavior, and withhold that information. Sometimes the motivation may be innocent — they're hoping you are the person who will get their relative straightened out.

Other times, however, they know all about the person's deficiencies, but they want you to take the person off their hands. In my research for my book, *Red Flags of Love Fraud*, one woman told me that on her wedding day, the mother of the groom came up to her and said, "He's your problem now."

And if your partner is estranged from his or her family, or doesn't allow you to meet the family, it could be another warning sign that he or she has something to hide.

Trust your instincts

So what do you do? How do you protect yourself from getting romantically involved with a psychopath?

Here's the best advice: Always trust your instincts. You have an internal warning system, and if you get a bad feeling about someone, pay attention.

So if you have a nagging suspicion, but haven't yet figured out why, it might help to take a look at your partner's relatives. Bad behavior somewhere on his or her family tree may help clarify your misgivings.

3 steps to prevent a sociopath from taking advantage of your vulnerabilities

"Is it really a vulnerability to respond to somebody (apparently) liking and desiring you? Is that not just a basic human need that we all want to have fulfilled?"

The Lovefraud reader Dorabella asked these questions on a story that I posted a couple of weeks ago, *The sociopath as your soul mate*. They are great questions. The answers are: Yes, it's a vulnerability to respond to someone desiring you, and yes, it's a basic human need. So although these are vulnerabilities, they are also normal human qualities.

To be human is to have vulnerabilities

A vulnerability is a weak point, and whenever we want something, that creates a weak point. Most of us want a romantic relationship, so if we don't have one, then yes, that is a vulnerability. But suppose you have a great relationship, but you want a more fulfilling job — then that's a vulnerability. Suppose you have a great relationship and a great job, but you want to make more money. That then becomes a vulnerability.

The list of possible vulnerabilities is endless — and normal. Vulnerabilities are not faults — they are part of the human experience. But vulnerabilities are also the openings that sociopaths exploit. Therefore, you need to understand your own vulnerabilities and how a sociopath may attempt to use them.

Here are three steps to protect yourself:

3 steps to prevent a sociopath from taking advantage of your vulnerabilities

1. Know your vulnerabilities

Are you lonely? Are you struggling to take care of your kids? Are you worried about money? These are all common vulnerabilities, and there are many, many more. A sociopath will snag you through your vulnerabilities. Therefore, you need to know what they are, so that you can pick up when you are being targeted.

How do you discover your vulnerabilities? Through self-reflection and paying attention to your inner dialog.

If you want a romantic partner and don't have one, that's an obvious vulnerability. But take a close look at your feelings on this issue. Do you feel like you're nothing without a partner? Do you feel like you're running out of time? The more desperate you feel, the easier it will be for a sociopath to target you.

Sit quietly with a pen and paper. Ask yourself, "What do I want? How badly do I want it?" Write down everything that comes to mind. You'll have a list of your vulnerabilities — which is the first step towards protecting yourself.

2. If your vulnerabilities are rooted in pain, heal them

As a human being, you've certainly endured disappointment and grief in your life. You may have also suffered real betrayal and abuse. These experiences create energies of pain and vulnerability within you — and sociopaths just seem to have radar to spot them.

Therefore, the best thing you can do to protect yourself from sociopaths is to work on healing your emotional pain. How do you do this? By allowing yourself to feel the pain, so you can let it go.

This means allowing yourself to cry, grieve or express anger about what happened to you. Sit quietly, permit memories of what happened rise to your awareness, and then feel the emotions of the experience.

This isn't pretty, so you'll want to do this either alone or with the help of a trusted therapist. And pain usually runs deep, so it will take time to access it all. But processing old emotions is absolutely worth the effort. Releasing old pain clears your internal vulnerabilities, so that sociopaths have less to latch on to. The healing work also enables you to feel happier and more peaceful.

3. If your vulnerabilities are targeted, listen to your intuition

Beware the person who seems to be the answer to your prayers. If someone sweeps into your life and tells you everything you want to hear, there's a chance that your vulnerabilities are being targeted.

Now is the time to pay attention to your intuition. If you are getting internal warnings that something is off about a person or a relationship, trust your instincts. Go on high alert, or end the involvement — even if you don't have proof of bad behavior. The time to pay attention to you intuition is before you have evidence of wrongdoing, not afterwards.

Being appropriately vulnerable

The truth is that any human relationship, especially a romantic partnership, requires a certain amount of vulnerability. You have to put yourself out there, take a chance, make a leap of faith. No one is perfect, so there are times that you will be disappointed in your relationships.

But by taking these steps, you can protect yourself from sociopaths who prey on vulnerabilities. Knowing exploiters and manipulators live among us, and understanding yourself, you'll be able to judge when it is safe to open your heart.

Why we fall for romance scams

Salon.com posted an article about online romance scams, *Facebook status: In a scam relationship,* by Tracy Clark-Flory. The scams run like this:

- Perp finds a target online.
- They communicate via email, text and sometimes phone.
- Perp proclaims undying love.
- Maybe perp sends flowers and stuffed teddy bears.
- Perp suddenly has a dire emergency and needs money.
- Target sends money, and keeps sending money until there's none left.

Apparently, romance scams — known as "love fraud," according to the article — are a growth industry. The story quoted a man named Rob who lost $14,000 to a woman he never met. He is now a volunteer for RomanceScams.org, which has counseled 50,000 people who believe they were swindled.

According to Salon:

> Many of the scammers are based in Nigeria, home of the infamous 419 email scam — love fraud is a much savvier twist on that old formula. "Scammers search chat rooms, dating sites, and social networking sites looking

for victims," warns the FBI's Internet Crime Complaint Center. "The principal group of victims is over 40 years old and divorced, widowed, elderly, or disabled, but all demographics are at risk." The perpetrators investigate the target by doing a Google search on their name and scouring their online profiles. "Once they have all that information, they create a character that is specific to you and your desires," Rob says. "In short, they create your dream mate, and they're very good at what they do, unfortunately."

The con artists frequently pose as soldiers serving in Afghanistan or Iraq. The problem has gotten so bad that the military has issued press releases warning people not to fall for soldiers asking for money so they can go on leave.

The Salon article explains how the scammers hook the targets, and the process is familiar to all of us who have been snagged by sociopaths: "The scammers get the target to reveal their most delicate feelings and secrets; and a sense of real intimacy often develops." And that's the reason the scams work—people are looking for love.

Plenty of readers commented on the article. Most of the comments expressed this view: Anyone who falls for an online romance scam is a complete idiot.

Why send money to Nigeria?

Lovefraud has heard from people who have fallen for these online scams. And even though I know how convincing sociopaths are, I must admit that these cases perplexed me.

Yes, I lost $227,000 to my con artist ex-husband. But he was physically with me. He looked me in the eye, made his promises, turned on the tears when necessary. He had sex with me, which released all that oxytocin, the trust hormone. He brought me around to his business friends, creating the illusion that he truly was an entrepreneur.

I know why I gave him my money. But why anyone would send money to a person they never met who lives in Nigeria?

I think the answer lies in the power of our own minds, and I'll take you through my reasoning.

Fantasy

First of all, it is very possible to have accepting, positive thoughts about people we've only met over the computer—just look at all the friendships that have developed here on Lovefraud. Taking this a step further to romance isn't difficult.

We may not really know what the person looks like or sounds like, because we've never met. But as I explain on the Lovefraud.com page called *Online Seduction,* we fill in any gaps in our knowledge about a potential romantic partner with fantasy:

> When you meet people in the real world, you notice their height, weight, grooming, voice, mannerisms — and immediately form conclusions about them. All of this information is missing in email correspondence. You can't see, smell or touch the person. You don't even really know if you're communicating with a man or a woman.
>
> So what do you do? You imagine the person is what you want him or her to be.

Essentially what happens is that in an online romance, we fall in love with our own fantasy. We create an image in our minds of what the person is, and how the person feels about us. And we believe it.

Oxytocin

I referred briefly to oxytocin above. This hormone is thought to be released during hugging, touching and orgasm in both men and women, and acts as a neurochemical in the brain. According to Wikipedia:

> Oxytocin evokes feelings of contentment, reductions in anxiety, and feelings of calmness and security around the mate. Many studies have already shown a correlation of oxytocin with human bonding, increases in trust, and decreases in fear.

Oxytocin serves a normal and important function in the human bonding process—it makes us feel calm and trusting with our mates. Nature probably gave us oxytocin so that we want to stay with our partners to raise children, thus helping the survival of the species.

But because it fosters trust, oxytocin can also help us get conned. Paul J. Zak explains this in a post on Psychology Today called, *How to run a con:*

> Social interactions engage a powerful brain circuit that releases the neurochemical oxytocin when we are trusted and induces a desire to reciprocate the trust we have been shown—even with strangers.
>
> The key to a con is not that you trust the conman, but that he shows he trusts you. Conmen ply their trade by appearing fragile or needing help, by seeming vulnerable. Because of oxytocin and its effect on other parts of the brain, we feel good when we help others—this is the basis for attachment to family and friends and cooperation with strangers. "I need your help" is a potent stimulus for action.

So, oxytocin doesn't necessarily require sex in order to be released. It can be triggered by other social interactions—perhaps even those conducted via electronic media.

Oxytocin is released in the brain and causes feelings of trust. But that isn't the only way in which love affects the brain. According to Dr. Helen Fisher, romantic love actually causes a rewiring of the brain. She also believes that romantic love is an addiction.

Brain action

You've probably heard of the "placebo effect." Physicians and researchers have long known that people in clinical trials of drugs frequently experience the benefits of the drug, even though they are taking the placebo. Because they believe they are taking the drug, they believe they will get better, and they do.

This is not just an imaginary improvement. According to an article called, *Placebo's power goes beyond the mind,* on MSNBC.MSN.com, "research shows that belief in a dummy treatment leads to changes in brain chemistry." In other words, belief can be just as strong as actual medication.

And here's another aspect of the brain: Research has found that the physical structure of the brain isn't nearly as static as once thought. As explained in, *How the brain rewires itself,* on Time.com:

> For decades, the prevailing dogma in neuroscience was that the adult human brain is essentially immutable, hardwired, fixed in form and function, so that by the time we reach adulthood we are pretty much stuck with what we have.
>
> But research in the past few years has overthrown the dogma. In its place has come the realization that the adult brain retains impressive powers of "neuroplasticity"—the ability to change its structure and function in response to experience.

The point, therefore, is that the brain is changeable, and it doesn't necessarily require drugs or a physical incident in order to change. Thoughts and beliefs have the power to change the brain.

Power of imagination

So where am I going with all this? Here is what I think may be happening in romance scams:

1. The perp contacts the target, gradually building the target's love and trust.
2. The target believes that the perp is real and they are in a romantic relationship.
3. Because of the target's belief, oxytocin is released in the brain, even though there is no physical touching.

4. The belief in love also rewires the brain, just as it does in a real relationship.
5. The target may even become addicted to the relationship.
6. The target is primed to be conned.

My theory, then, is that in an online romance scam, we believe we are in a true romantic relationship. Our belief causes all the same brain changes that a real world relationship causes. Because of the power of our imaginations, we may be just as susceptible to online scams as we are to real life scams.

Come to think of it, this is probably why we fall for the real life scams. We believe the love is true, even though it isn't.

5 reasons why you can hook up with multiple sociopaths

Lovefraud recently received the following inquiry from a reader whom we'll call "Leslie-Marie."

>Is it not uncommon for people to have several relationships with sociopaths and/or narcissists throughout their life?
>
>I am wondering if you would do a write up on this topic as I find it so difficult to explain to others. They look at me in such disbelief, as if I'm making it up. It would be nice to have something to back me up. I can count 7 at least that I am certain of and have been closely involved with.
>
>Would you also consider explaining how this cycle can continue and what is it about us that attracts them or why we are attracted to them?

Donna Andersen responds

Yes, Leslie-Marie, it is certainly possible to find yourself in relationships with multiple sociopaths. Here's why:

1. Millions of them live among us

All of us are surrounded by sociopaths. Depending on which official estimates you look at, people with antisocial, narcissistic or borderline personality disorders, or psychopathy, make up 12% to 16% of the population. In the United States, that's 38 million to 51 million people.

Now, these are only the people who are disordered enough to be clinically diagnosed. There are also people who have some disordered traits, but not all of them. Believe me, you do not want to be involved with them either.

I've never heard an estimate of how many people may be moderately disordered, but it's probably at least the same as the number who are fully disordered. That may mean that 76 million to 102 million people in the U.S. are moderately or fully disordered.

Disordered people are everywhere — in all demographic groups and all walks of life. We are all going to run across them.

2. You may cross paths with high numbers of sociopaths

Sociopaths are absolutely everywhere. But I can think of some situations in which there may be a higher concentration of sociopaths than usual. If you deal with these situations, you may come across them more often.

Criminals. This is obvious. Almost all criminals meet the criteria for antisocial personality disorder (This is one of the problems with the diagnostic criteria — many experts say they are too broad.) I hope this isn't the case, but if you have criminals, drug dealers or gang members in your life, you are likely encounter a lot of sociopaths.

Stockbrokers and money managers. Dr. Robert Hare, author of *Without Conscience,* once said that if he ran out of psychopaths to study in prison, he'd look for them at the stock exchange. Psychopaths love taking big risks with other people's money. In fact, one researcher believes that the global financial collapse of 2008 was caused by psychopathic money managers taking extreme risks.

Corporate executives. Dr. Hare believes that about 1% of the general population meets his definition of a psychopath. But he conducted research among corporate executives, and discovered that 3.5% of them met the criteria. That means there are 3.5 times as many psychopaths in corporate offices than there are on the streets.

Online hookups. I said that 12% to 16% of the population is disordered. That includes the population of the Internet. Sociopaths love the Internet. They search for targets 24/7; they pretend to be whomever they want; they can look for hookups all over the world. In one Lovefraud survey, 23% of people said they met the sociopath online. It was the most common way that people met sociopaths.

3. You didn't fully recover from previous sociopathic partners

To answer your question about how the cycle continues, betrayal by a sociopath leaves deep emotional wounds. You are hurt, angry, disappointed, ashamed and grieving. At least you should be, but perhaps you didn't allow yourself to feel the depths of your pain. Instead, you picked yourself up, dusted yourself off and got out there again.

What happens? The negative energy from previous betrayals may still be inside you, festering. Sociopaths have radar for this pain. They home in on it, and promise to make your pain go away. You fall for it. The relationship is good for a while — but then it all goes bad, and you feel worse than ever.

This is why it is so important to fully recover from betrayals, even if it means you stop dating for a while. You really need to take time to heal. When you do, you can attract much healthier romantic partners.

4. Growing up around disordered people

I can't tell you how many people I've spoken to about their disordered partners who realized that they got involved with someone who was just like their mother, father or someone else from their childhood.

The fact is that if you endured any kind of abuse as a child, even emotional or psychological abuse, it makes you more susceptible to sociopaths later on in life. When you're a child, you don't have the tools to deal with the pain, anger, disappointment, shame and grief inflicted upon you by adults. So you bottle it up inside. Again, sociopaths sense your vulnerability and use it to hook you.

5. You know what sociopaths look like

Leslie-Marie, I'm willing to bet that the people who look at you with such disbelief have also been involved with sociopaths.

Now that I know what a personality disorder is, I can definitely say I dated at least two disordered men before my sociopathic husband. The first was a garden-variety con man who took several thousand dollars from me.

The second may have had borderline personality disorder. He was doting, until I told him I didn't want to be involved with a gambler. He turned on me with such ferocity that I was stunned. Then he did the crying routine, telling me how he really didn't mean it. Looking back, it was classic abusive behavior.

So Leslie-Marie, the difference between you and your friends may simply be that you know what a sociopath looks like and they don't. I hope they take the time to educate themselves. It could save them a lot of heartache.

Will emotional abuse become physical abuse?

If you are targeted by a sociopath, you will endure emotional abuse.

Sociopaths — meaning people with antisocial, narcissistic, borderline, histrionic or psychopathic personality disorders — live their lives by manipulating and exploiting others. So if you have any kind of extensive or ongoing involvement with a sociopath, you will be manipulated, deceived and betrayed. It's just a matter of how badly.

Manipulation, deceit and betrayal are all forms of emotional abuse.

Why? Because society runs on trust, and sociopaths violate trust. When the trust you place in someone is violated, you suffer an emotional wound.

But will emotional abuse become physical abuse? The answer is, maybe.

What is emotional abuse?

There is no official, concise definition of emotional abuse. Typically, emotional abuse is defined via specific examples of offensive behavior, such as:

- Manipulating your emotions
- Lying
- Bullying
- Saying you are unattractive

- Flirting with others and cheating
- Silent treatment
- Changing what he/she wants
- Refusing to offer support when you need it
- Trying to convince others that you are crazy
- Humiliating you
- Shaming you
- Blaming you
- Making you feel guilty
- Intimidation
- Minimizing hurtful behavior
- Revealing private information about you
- Threatening suicide

So essentially, emotional abuse is any ongoing, intentional behavior that makes you feel bad.

Keep in mind that emotional abuse doesn't just happen in the context of romantic relationships:

- Sociopathic parents always emotionally abuse their children — they are incapable of providing appropriate love and concern for their children's development.
- Sociopathic siblings torment their brothers and sisters. In fact, sociopaths typically take advantage of any family member who has something they want.
- Sociopathic bosses may shame, blame and rage at employees.
- Sociopathic employees may undermine co-workers and stab them in the back.
- Sociopathic neighbors may harass anyone in the community.
- Sociopathic friends may act more like parasites than friends.

Will emotional abuse become physical abuse?

Whether emotional abuse becomes physical abuse depends on

Will emotional abuse become physical abuse?

the nature of the relationship and the particular sociopath. Typically, emotional abuse becomes physical abuse behind closed doors. So that means it happens most often in intimate relationships and families.

Some sociopaths do start out with emotional abuse and later escalate to physical abuse. Essentially they are exerting more and more power and control over you.

Often, they train you to accept the abuse. They do this by engaging in relatively mild abuse at first, and then gradually ramping up the negative behavior.

For emotional abuse, they may start out by making a critical remark, and when you take offense, say that they're sorry, they didn't mean it. The jabs may slowly become meaner, or the lies more blatant, until the behavior escalates to the silent treatment and threats.

Somewhere along the line, the abuse may become physical. Again, at first it may be a slight push, followed by an apology — it was an accident. Then the sociopath may hit you harder. If you stay and tolerate it, the next incident is more violent. It may continue to escalate, until you possibly end up in the hospital or dead.

Many sociopaths do not engage in physical abuse

Many sociopaths never lift a hand in physical abuse — all of their destructive behavior is emotional abuse (including psychological and verbal abuse). Some people will stay with someone who is tormenting them emotionally because, "at least he (or she) isn't hitting me."

Emotional abuse is never acceptable. In fact, it is often more damaging than physical abuse.

Why? One reason is because you can't get any support. When people don't see cuts and bruises, they often don't take you seriously. This is especially true when the sociopath presents as charming and helpful in the community or workplace, so people cannot imagine that he or she is a monster at home.

Another reason is because you begin to doubt yourself. You wonder what you are doing wrong that makes the sociopath treat you so badly — not realizing that the answer is nothing.

Seduced by a Sociopath

If you feel that a partner or family member is becoming abusive, either emotionally or physically, do not allow it to escalate. The longer you accept the sociopath's apologies and promises not to do it again, the more you will lose confidence, your belief in yourself and your ability to end the involvement.

Abuse wears you down. Don't get so low that you can't get out of the situation.

Sociopaths use our self-image against us

We all have a mental picture of ourselves. We may think of ourselves as smart, kind, creative, professional, competent or loving. We may also have negative views of ourselves, such as disorganized, overweight, temperamental, fearful or lazy. Generally, our overall self-image is a collection of what we consider to be our assets and liabilities.

According to the Cleveland Clinic, this mental picture is learned. They write:

> Self-image is a product of learning. Early childhood influences, such as parents and caregivers, significantly influence our self-image. They are mirrors reflecting back to us an image of ourselves. Our experiences with others — such as teachers, friends, and family — add to the image in the mirror. Relationships reinforce what we think and feel about ourselves.

Our self-image may be accurate or distorted. We may think more highly of our talents we really deserve, or we may be beating ourselves up unnecessarily.

Whatever our personal view of ourselves, sociopaths find ways to exploit it.

Boosting our self image

When sociopaths are trying to hook us and reel us in, they

shower us with compliments and flattery. They talk about how they feel so much in common with us. They agree with our views and opinions.

In short, we feel like the sociopaths recognize our good points.

They also say things to make us feel better about our weaknesses. For example, if we feel that we could stand to lose some weight, sociopaths reassure us that we simply offer "more to love."

What do all these tactics have in common? They boost our self-image.

That's in the beginning of the involvement. Once we're hooked, however, sociopaths target our self-image in other ways.

Within the relationship

Whenever there's a conflict with sociopaths, a typical tactic is for them to accuse us of traits and behaviors that run counter to how we think about ourselves.

For example, if we turn down a request for money, they may call us greedy or stingy, when we've already been more than generous with them.

If we don't agree to do something that they want us to do, they may call us self-centered. The truth may be that we do everything we can to accommodate others.

And here's a big one: If we disagree on anything, they say that we don't love really them — when we love this person more than we've ever loved anyone.

So what happens? We work to prove the sociopath wrong. We try to convince the sociopaths that we aren't what they are saying about us.

It's a brilliant approach by the sociopaths. We can't stand the idea that they have such a negative view of us. So what's the fastest way to change their mind? Agreeing with what they want.

Added bonus for the sociopath: Not only do they get what they want, but they also increase their control over us.

Within the community

Long before we may have any inkling that sociopaths are thinking about discarding us, they launch the smear campaign.

Sociopaths use our self-image against us

They start talking behind our backs. They spread stories about us, such as they suspect we're doing drugs or cheating on them.

One of the their favorite lies is that we are mentally unbalanced. They say this to friends and family, usually feigning tremendous concern, so that everyone believes what they say.

Much later, when we decide we've had enough of their exploitation, we try to tell our friends and family what has really been going on in our relationship — and no one believes us! They've already been warned that we are cheating, drug-addicted psychos!

Why is the smear campaign so devastating? Because it attacks who we think we are.

We know that we did not do what the sociopaths say we did. We are not who the sociopaths say we are. The sociopaths' lies offend our self-image.

What to do

The best thing you can do, either before tangling with a sociopath, or while recovering from their manipulation, is to work on developing a strong, positive self-image.

Plenty of experts have written about building your self-image or self-esteem (essentially the same thing). Here are tips from the Cleveland Clinic:

Specific steps to foster a positive self-image

- Take a self-image inventory
- Make a list of your positive qualities
- Ask significant others to describe your positive qualities
- Define personal goals and objectives that are reasonable and measurable
- Confront thinking distortions
- Identify and explore the impact of childhood labels
- Refrain from comparing yourself to others
- Develop your strengths
- Learn to love yourself

- Give positive affirmations
- Remember that you are unique
- Remember how far you have come

At the same time, recognize that sociopaths intentionally target your self-image, and exploit the way you view yourself to get what they want.

So look carefully at how your views of yourself may have been influenced by the sociopaths. It may be time to change your mind about your self-image.

Getting over that amazing 'chemistry'

Sooner or later, those of us who are romantically involved, or have been romantically involved, with sociopaths and other exploiters recognize that the relationship is bad for us and must end. Although we know this intellectually, often we still feel incredible attraction, even love, for the individual. How do we break the emotional attachment?

For example, Lovefraud received the following letter:

> I am single, and I think I was with someone very narcissistic, if not outright sociopathic. The thing is, even though I am no longer with him (and he did not get to my finances), he broke my heart.
> My question is, how do you get over him? I have tried to date others, but no man has compared with the chemistry and (you know, all the rest) that I had with the narcissist. I have a man now who truly loves me, and we are soul mates. I just don't have that "sizzle" with him that I did with the one who was bad for me. Do you think I should "settle" for the good, honest man? I mean, I am attracted to him; it's just not the mad passion like the narcissist brought out.

Many, many readers have told Lovefraud that getting over relationships with sociopaths (narcissists, etc.) is much more difficult than getting over other relationships that they've had. The reasons for this are complicated, and are rooted in both normal human psychology and the sociopath's pathology.

The seduction

The first thing to understand is that sociopaths engage in seduction. This is significantly different from a normal dating relationship.

When two relatively healthy people begin dating, they are both testing the waters. They are spending time with each other to see if they like each other enough, or have enough in common, or get along well enough, to keep going. Yes, one party may be more interested than the other, but neither of them has made a decision.

In contrast, sociopaths purposely and consciously seduce their targets. They lavish the person with attention. They want to know everything about the target, they call and text constantly, they shower the person with gifts large and small. Sociopaths move fast, and quickly begin talking about love, commitment and marriage. This is called love bombing.

For most of us, the only experience we've ever had with this level of attention is in a fairytale. We are swept off our feet, caught up in the intensity, the magic, of Prince or Princess Charming. We've heard all those stories of "love at first sight," and hope that it's finally happened to us. We think it's real.

Here's what you need to understand: The sociopath's extraordinary pursuit is never about love. It is about predation. You are or have something that the sociopath wants—at least for the moment. Despite what the sociopath says, his or her interest in you is not about building a relationship or future together. It's about acquiring a possession.

The sex adventure

Sociopaths, both men and women, are hard-wired for sex. They have high levels of testosterone, and a strong appetite for stimulation. These two facts are probably responsible for the "animal magnetism" that we sense with them.

But that's only the beginning. Sociopaths are often extraordinarily energetic and proficient lovers — at least technically. Because of their tremendous sexual appetite, they start young and have a lot of partners, so they quickly become experienced. And, because they have no shame, they feel no inhibitions. In fact, they frequently want to push their partners' boundaries.

Is this passion? No—it's boredom. Sociopaths quickly tire of the same old thing, and want new sexual adventures. Getting the target to go along with their desires offers two types of rewards: They enjoy new modes of stimulation. And, they manipulate the partners. This is especially fun if the partner initially resists the demands.

The sex connection

From Nature's point of view, of course, the purpose of sex is propagation—the continuation of the human species. Nature wants children to survive, and the best chance of that happening is when parents stay together to care for them.

Therefore, sexual intimacy causes changes in the brain that contribute to bonding between the partners. One agent for doing this is oxytocin, a neurotransmitter sometimes called the "love hormone."

Oxytocin is released during sexual orgasm, and, in women, in childbirth and nursing. According to Wikipedia, here's what the hormone does:

> Oxytocin evokes feelings of contentment, reductions in anxiety, and feelings of calmness and security around the mate. In order to reach full orgasm, it is necessary that brain regions associated with behavioral control, fear and anxiety are deactivated; which allows individuals to let go of fear and anxiety during sexual arousal. Many studies have already shown a correlation of oxytocin with human bonding, increases in trust, and decreases in fear.

So during sex, your brain is being flooded with calmness, trust and contentment, and fear and anxiety are alleviated. If you're involved in a true loving and committed relationship, this contributes to bonding, which is fine and healthy.

Sociopaths, however, do not bond in the same way that healthy people do. Although we don't know if oxytocin works differently in sociopaths, or perhaps doesn't work at all, we do know that sociopaths are deficient in their ability to love. So while the healthy partner develops a love bond, the sociopath does not.

The addiction

A love bond is created by pleasure, and during the seduction phase of the relationship, the sociopath generates extreme pleasure for the target. However, addiction research has discovered that although pleasure is required to form a bond, pleasure is not required to maintain it. Even when a relationship starts to get rocky, normal people still feel bonded. Again, this is Nature's way of keeping people together. If parents split up at the first sign of trouble, the survival of children would be in doubt.

Sooner or later, of course, relationships with sociopaths get rocky. Perhaps the sociopath engages in cheating, stealing or abuse. The sociopath's actions create fear and anxiety in the target. But instead of driving the target away from the sociopath, anxiety and fear actually strengthen the psychological love bond.

So what do the targets do? They turn to the sociopaths for relief. The sociopaths may apologize profusely and promise to change their hurtful ways, reassuring the targets. The targets, feeling bonded to the sociopaths, want to believe the reassurances, so they do. Then the two people have sex, which reinforces the bond again.

From the target's point of view, the relationship becomes a vicious circle of bonding, anxiety, fear, relief, sex and further bonding. The longer it goes on, the harder it is for the target to escape.

The result: For the target, the love bond becomes an addiction.

Vulnerability

How is this possible? How do targets get into this predicament?

Often, targets are primed for sociopathic relationships due to trauma that they have already experienced in their lives. As children, they may have suffered physical, emotional, psychological or sexual abuse from family members, authority figures or others. Or, the targets may have already experienced exploitative relationships, such as domestic violence, from which they have not recovered.

These abusive experiences create "trauma bonds." As a result, abuse and exploitation feel normal to a target.

For healing to occur, targets need to look honestly into themselves and into their histories, finding the root of the issue. Was there a prior relationship that made you vulnerable to a sociopath?

Recovery

So, to answer the original question in the letter, how do you get over the sociopath?

First of all, you need to understand that what you are feeling is not chemistry or love. You are feeling addiction and a pathological love bond — the trauma bond.

Healing requires conscious effort. The book called *The Betrayal Bond*, by Patrick J. Carnes, Ph.D., is an excellent resource for doing this. Carnes writes:

> Once a person has been part of our lives, the ripples remain, even though we have no further contact. In that sense a relationship continues even though we may consciously exorcise it from our conscious contact. Once you understand that principle, a shift will occur in all of your contact with others.

If the relationship was toxic, as in a traumatic bond, the relationship must go through a transformation, since it will always be with you. You do not need to be in contact with the person to change the nature of the relationship. You can change how you perceive it. You can change how it impacts you.

How do you do this? You commit to facing the reality of the relationship—all of it. Trauma tends to distort perception—you want to focus the good memories and forget about the bad ones.

You must force yourself to deal with the truth of the experience—including the betrayal.

If you're still feeling the tug of the pathological relationship, *The Betrayal Bond* includes information and exercises that can help you break free. (My book, *Love Fraud,* describes an alternative path to recovery.)

And to the Lovefraud letter-writer: Do not confuse drama with love. Accepting a good, honest man is not "settling." It is the foundation of a healthy relationship.

You can move forward.

A sociopath claims, 'We are evolution's next step'

Do sociopaths know what they are? Many, many Lovefraud readers ask me this question. The short answer is that some of them do and some of them don't.

The man who sent me the following email certainly has insight into his own personality:

> I would like to thank you for making your videos — they have given me an insight into how you people recognize us. WE are not to blame for your shortcomings because you are weak minded and foolish enough to be taken advantage of. We are evolutions next step — we don't allow silly emotions to cloud our judgments. In fact we use our advantage for survival because we are natures next course. I know I sound very narcissistic and apologize for that but if you are so proud and concerned and attached to your emotions why not allow someone to make you feel like a queen for something as worldly as money? We give you what you are missing just as all of the world ecosystem has since the beginning of time. It's funny how we have been so easily classified and even now as I attempt to alter myself in order to become unparallel to descriptions of us, I find it very difficult to even perceive. I would like to boast of my strategic victories over hearts but I would fear you making another video and making this game more difficult, of course it would make it much more challenging

and pleasurable when enjoying the hunt.

This email is a great example of the sociopathic perspective, whether or not individual sociopaths are aware of it. Lest we forget, here is how sociopaths view themselves, the rest of us, and the world:

1. Sociopaths are superior beings, and everyone else is a mark.
2. If marks are dumb enough to be conned, they get what they deserve.
3. Marks deserve to be targeted because of their stupid emotions and consciences.
4. Emotions and consciences are useful in marks, because they can be exploited.
5. Exploitation is a perfectly reasonable way for sociopaths to get what they want.

This is why there is no rehabilitation for sociopaths. They do not feel that they have a disorder; rather, sociopaths believe they have an evolutionary competitive advantage.

Or, for those sociopaths who don't have the intelligence or education to analyze their place in the world, they're simply content the way they are and see no need for change.

What if you see some signs of a sociopath, but not all of them?

Editor's note: This is Part 1 of a two-part inquiry that Lovefraud received from a reader whom we'll call "Carlotta."

I recently met and "dated" a man who turned out to be a sociopath. When I first met him I used your list of 10 signs to help me determine what I needed to do to protect myself if he should turn out to be a sociopath or worse.

I wasn't too worried about him, because initially I noticed he had only 3 of the 10 traits. The notation with your list says if they have most or all of the traits they may be a sociopath. He turned out to be a sociopath, so now I wonder if the specific traits they have are more telling than the number of traits they have.

In the case of the man I was dating, it was immediately apparent the following applied to him:

#2. Sudden Soul Mates
#4. Love Bombing
#8. Moves Fast to Hookup

However, it wasn't apparent to me until dating him 6 days out of 7 that the following also applied:

#6. Lies and Gaps in the Story.

I feel lucky that I had your list to refer to because I was able to keep my emotional distance while getting to "know" him (if such a thing is possible with sociopaths). I checked his court records online and they were quite telling, once I realized he was telling lies and leaving gaps. After I asked a few pointed questions he discontinued contact with me. I feel that a blessing since I didn't need to initiate the disconnect myself.

I'm a little concerned that in describing your list, you state that if the person has most or all of the traits. Initially I saw only 3 traits and after a week only one more. I don't know how long it would have taken for any other traits to show up, or if there are more traits that fit him. I don't want any other women to think that they're safe because the person they're dating only has 3 or 4 of the traits that show up within a week.

Is it possible you could add clarification to your list about which traits show up first or how long it may take to see some of the traits? Could you possibly list which traits are more telling or are they all equally telling?

Donna Andersen responds

Carlotta, thank you so much for your questions. First of all, for the benefit of all Lovefraud readers, here is the complete list of the Red Flags of Love Fraud:

1. **Charisma and charm.** They're smooth talkers, always have an answer, never miss a beat. They seem to be very exciting.
2. **Sudden soul mates.** They figure out what you want, make themselves into that person, then tell you that your relationship was "meant to be."
3. **Sexual magnetism.** If you feel intense attraction, if your physical relationship is unbelievable, it may be their excess testosterone.
4. **Love bombing.** You're showered with attention and adoration. They want to be with you all the time. They call, text and e-mail constantly.
5. **Blames others for everything.** Nothing is ever their fault. They always have an excuse. Someone else causes their problems.

What if you see some signs of a sociopath, but not all of them?

6. **Lies and gaps in the story.** You ask questions, and the answers are vague. They tell stupid lies. They tell outrageous lies. They lie when they'd make out better telling the truth.
7. **Intense eye contact.** Call it the predatory stare. If you get a chill down your spine when they look at you, pay attention.
8. **Moves fast to hook up.** It's a whirlwind romance. They quickly proclaim their true love. They want to move in together or get married quickly.
9. **Pity play.** They appeal to your sympathy. They want you to feel sorry for their abusive childhood, psychotic ex, incurable disease or financial setbacks.
10. **Jekyll and Hyde personality.** One minute they love you; the next minute they hate you. Their personality changes like flipping a switch.

Seeing the signs may take time

You alluded to one of the important points about spotting a sociopath: You may not see all the signs right away.

Sociopaths are sometimes able to maintain the charade of an attentive lover for quite a long time — especially while they are reeling in a target. So let's take a look at the list to determine what you are likely to see first.

As research for my book, *Red Flags of Love Fraud — 10 signs you're dating a sociopath*, I conducted an Internet survey that was completed by more than 1,300 people. According to the results, the Number One Red Flag, seen by 91.5% of respondents, was:

1. Charisma and charm

This is something you are likely to see immediately. That's often why the person catches your attention in the first place and seems so appealing — he or she is so charismatic and charming.

However, just because a person is charismatic and charming, it doesn't mean he or she is a sociopath. Plenty of people who have these traits are also able to love authentically.

You also spotted three other Red Flags that are likely to appear

quickly:
- **2. Sudden soul mates**
- **4. Love bombing**
- **8. Moves fast to hook up**

The problem with the traits that we've discussed so far is that there is nothing inherently wrong with them. In fact, who wouldn't want to find a romantic partner who was charismatic, shared values and interests, was crazy about you, and wants to be with you all the time?

These traits could describe love at first sight. And love at first sight is a real, albeit rare, phenomenon — I personally know of several couples who met, immediately fell in love, married, and stayed happily married for a very long time.

That's why the following traits are so important:
- **5. Blames others for everything**
- **9. Pity play**

Even while someone is showering you with attention and trying to spend as much time with you as possible, he or she may exhibit these negative traits. They may have an excuse for all of their problems — usually that someone else screwed up or did them wrong. And, they may tell you sob stories, trying to get you to feel sorry for them.

These traits, therefore, may be the first clues that the person may be disordered.

Two of the traits on the list are on physical in nature:
- **4. Sexual magnetism**
- **7. Intense eye contact**

Fully 78% of my survey respondents said that sexual magnetism was a characteristic of their involvement with a sociopath. Many, many people have told me that the sex they had with the sociopath was the best they ever experienced.

Intense eye contact was not as prevalent — it was noted by 59% of respondents. But this is an important sign, because it is the only physical characteristic that you may be able to observe.

This is the critical warning sign:
- **6. Lies and gaps in the story**

All sociopaths lie. They tell big lies, little lies, stupid lies. They

What if you see some signs of a sociopath, but not all of them?

sometimes lie when they are better off telling the truth.

But the whole point about lying is that you don't know it is happening. Research shows that people can spot a lie only about 53% of the time — not much better than flipping a coin.

Many people have told me that it took them years to figure out that the sociopath was lying. Why? Because sociopaths lie so convincingly. Then they lie to cover up their previous lies. And many of them can keep all the lies straight.

So although lying is the cardinal sign of a sociopath, this behavior can be difficult to spot.

Finally, here's the last trait:

10. Jekyll and Hyde personality

Some sociopaths can fly into a sudden rage over something that you feel is a minor misunderstanding, or over nothing at all. And then, after the sociopath viciously lashes out at you, he or she acts like nothing happened.

It is unlikely that you'll see this trait right away. When sociopaths are reeling you in, they're on their best behavior. If you see this trait at all, it will probably be directed towards someone else, not you.

But one day, if you stay involved with this person, it will be directed toward you. So I view this trait as final confirmation. If you've seen the other Red Flags, but you're still not sure about the individual, having the person turn on you should help you make up your mind.

Real or faked

So why do I say that you need to see all of the Red Flags to suspect that someone is a sociopath? Because I don't want you to be suspicious of every charming, sexy, potential partner who shares your interests and seems to be crazy about you. There are authentic people out there, and maybe you have, in fact, found a keeper.

The problem, of course, is that sociopaths have learned how to imitate a smitten lover. So your challenge is to discern whether the head-over-heels affection you're seeing is real or fake.

That's where the other signs come it. If you are also seeing the negative traits, be careful.

Partial problems

Another point to keep in mind is that sociopathy is both a syndrome and a continuum.

A syndrome is a collection of traits of behaviors that tend to be seen together. Any particular sociopath may have some of the traits of the disorder, but not all of them.

Sociopathy is also a continuum. This means that a particular sociopath may have any of the traits to greater or lesser degrees.

The bottom line is that sociopaths are not all the same, they may have different combinations of traits, and some are more disordered than others. Some people may be only partially affected — not disordered enough that a clinician would diagnose a personality disorder.

However, if a person has some of the negative traits of the disorder, but is not a full-blown, diagnosable sociopath, you still do not want this individual as a romantic partner.

Three steps to staying safe

Here's how to protect yourself:

1. Know that sociopaths exist. If you're reading Lovefraud, you have this one covered.
2. Know the Red Flags of Love Fraud. I hope that this article has helped you.
3. Trust your instincts. This is the best thing you can do to protect yourself. If you ever get a gut feeling, intuition or instinct that there is something wrong with an individual, pay attention.

Your instincts are designed to keep you out of danger. Listen to them.

Are sociopaths opportunists?

Editor's note: This is Part 2 of a two-part inquiry from the Lovefraud reader whom we call "Carlotta."

On another note, a personal concern of mine is that I may have chosen that sociopath, not the other way around. I was walking through a department store and out of the corner of my eye I saw a man standing still facing me. I looked up and he was smiling at me. I smiled back. Then we walked in separate directions. But later we passed one another in a different area of the store. I was lost and he was again just standing there smiling at me. I smiled and asked if he was lost like me. We then talked for a long time and exchanged cell numbers, etc.

Here are my concerns. Did I choose him or did he choose me? Do sociopaths wait like an eel in a cave, for the right time and victim to pass within their reach? Can sociopaths be THAT patient? Are some or all sociopaths opportunists, rather than movers and shakers? Did that sociopath see me as a victim or possible victim from a distance before we even spoke? Because I don't understand what happened, thinking about those questions rattles my nerves and makes me leery of speaking to any strangers.

Any insight you can give me about what happened and why is appreciated.

Donna Andersen responds

Yes, sociopaths are opportunists. People with antisocial personality disorder or psychopathy typically go through their days, and their lives, with their eyes open for people to exploit.

If a "mark" crosses their path, they'll pounce.

Here's what happens when a sociopath meets you:

- The sociopath sizes you up to determine if you have something that he or she wants.
- Then, the sociopath looks for your vulnerabilities.
- Finally, the sociopath figures out a way, using your vulnerabilities, to get what he or she wants.

Everyone is a potential victim

So did the sociopath see you as a victim from a distance? In a sense, yes, but you shouldn't feel like you are weak or vulnerable, because sociopaths sees everyone as a potential victim.

People who are antisocial or psychopathic look at the world as predators and prey. They are the predators; everyone else is the prey.

You escaped

Carlotta, instead of being rattled, you should congratulate yourself. You recognized enough of the Red Flags of Love Fraud to end your involvement with this man in six days! That's terrific!

We are not going to be able to go through life completely avoiding all sociopaths. There are simply too many of them, and they are everywhere.

But we can avoid becoming seriously damaged by them. That's exactly what you did. You should be proud!

The sociopath's isolation campaign: Keeping you from the people you love

A sociopath looks deep into your eyes. "I never loved anyone like I love you," he says. "We are so special together. People will never understand why we're so attracted to each other. They say we shouldn't be together, but they're just jealous about the intensity of our love. Love can overcome anything, you know. It's you and me against the world, kid!"

With words like these, sociopaths launch one of their most important strategies: Isolating you from friends and family.

It doesn't seem that way at first. In the beginning, sociopaths want to be with you all the time. They proclaim that they are so wrapped up in you that they can't bear to be apart, and it feels flattering to be so desired. Slowly, this morphs into the sociopath always wanting to know where you are, which morphs into jealousy if you spend time with anyone else, including your family and long-time friends.

They want you all to themselves. Not because they love you, despite their flowery proclamations. It's because they want to control you.

Isolation tactics

Sociopaths employ many tactics to keep you from the people who love you. Here are a few of them:

- Sociopaths intercept phone calls and mail, and "neglect" to give you messages.

- Sociopaths purposely insult or pick fights with your family and friends, so that the people you know find it easier to just stay away.
- Sociopaths say they are "protecting" you from the people who want to drive the two of you apart.
- If you do see your family and friends, sociopaths call and text constantly, interrupting your visit and making others uncomfortable.
- Sociopaths make up lies about what friends and family are saying about you.
- Sociopaths lie to family and friends about you, trying to turn them against you.
- Sociopaths rage at you when you leave, and rage again when you come home.
- Eventually, sociopaths forbid you to have contact with family and friends.

My experience

I remember how James Montgomery worked it with me. At first, he was solicitous towards my family. But nine months after we met, and after we married, my family was suspicious of him, and my brother wanted to run a credit check. I knew Montgomery's credit was bad—he'd already told me so, put expenses on my credit cards, and wiped out my savings.

I informed Montgomery, in anger, about my family's concern. His first reaction was to tearfully ask if I wanted him to leave. Believing that my husband was working towards out mutual good, and wanting to get my money back as he consistently promised, I said no, we'd stay married.

But from that point on, he used the incident to drive a wedge between me and my family. He refused to attend my other brother's wedding reception, stating that he wouldn't go where he wasn't welcome. He raged that I was an adult, I'd made my decision to marry him, and in some places people could be sued for interfering with a marriage. He disparaged my family and friends.

So as life with my husband became worse and worse, there was no one for me to talk to about it.

The sociopath's isolation campaign: Keeping you from the people you love

Pleas from family members

Isolation takes away your support system. When your contact with other people is limited, it enables the sociopaths to control the information you receive. And the more control they exercise, the more you lose your sense of self.

Periodically, Lovefraud receives distraught calls and emails from people who have lost sons, daughters or other family members to sociopaths. They want their loved ones to return, but the victims refuse. The sociopaths have so much power over them that it seems like the victims are lost forever.

The sad thing is that frequently, very little can be done until the victim himself or herself is ready to end the involvement. Psychologically, Dr. Liane Leedom explains, the victim has to take on his or her own distress. If family and friends are distressed, they are carrying what should be the victim's emotional burden. For healing to begin, it's up to the victim to start making a change.

For more information on this, read Dr. Leedom's article on Lovefraud, *How can I get my _____ away from the psychopathic con artist?*

Find the strength

Are you in this position? Has a sociopath separated you from all your friends and family, so that you feel like you have nowhere to go?

Know this: If the sociopath is the one telling you that your friends and family want nothing to do with you, that the sociopath is the only one who loves you, there's an excellent chance that he or she is lying.

If you've always had a good, or at least decent, relationship with friends and family, they're probably worried sick about you, and willing to help you escape the prison built by the sociopath.

All you need to do is find the strength to contact them.

Sociopaths use our own dreams to seduce us

Not long ago, a woman from the Philippines contacted Lovefraud. She had been involved in a long-distance relationship (LDR) with an American man whom she met over the Internet. This woman, we'll call her Juanita, fell in love with the guy, even though she never met him in person.

Juanita sent her story to Lovefraud—a shortened version is reproduced below. But first, a bit of background. Juanita is separated from her husband and has a child. Although she'd like to find a new husband, she is trapped, because divorce is not legal in the Philippines.

Looking for companionship, she turned to the Internet — which is what thousands of Filipinas do. In fact, the mail-order bride business, matching men from America, Europe and Australia with women from the Philippines, is booming.

Apparently some Filipinas have found love via the Internet, but not Juanita. Here is her story:

Bewitched from afar

> I met G online over a year ago. I've resorted to this kind of medium because I'm hoping to find someone who could be a good husband and father to my child. Not a few women here in the Philippines have met their current partners through the Internet.
>
> Although we only saw each other through pictures, some videos, and webcam meeting, G managed to deceive

me not only through the chat screen, but also through daily phone talks that got me addicted. And although he didn't ask for money from me, I did buy and send him stuff as my way of taking care of him. He did his share, too. But thinking about his efforts, it's undeniable that he did those to earn my trust back after I caught him cheating online the first time. I should have learned my lesson from that, but I opted to give him a second chance because I loved him.

[The police arrested the American for chatting with a minor online and then arranging to meet her.]

Throughout his jail time for almost four months, G and I didn't correspond. When he got out, he emailed me, apologizing for what he did and hoping that I'd still talk to him. I accepted his apology, thinking that his incarceration could have reformed him. And even if he said he had no intention of rekindling our failed affair, he wooed me back, saying he's learned his lessons and would make it up to me.

Our "second chance" lasted for almost 10 months. He proposed marriage a week before his scheduled jury trial and sent an engagement ring that he crafted himself. He asked that I let him talk to my parents so he could tell them his intention and our plan. This move really made me think that he's a reformed man.

With our daily phone talks, I didn't think he would go online again to chat with other women. And thinking about it, he must be laughing so hard whenever he gets to make me believe that he's being faithful with me—and that he truly loved me.

I discovered that he made another Yahoo account and replied via email to Filipinas who posted personal ads on craigslist. He was able to chat with other Filipinas again and lured three or five of them to have online LDRs with him. He even e-mailed a female best friend who has been in love with him, asking her who would he pick among the 11 Filipinas he was able to snag online.

I felt so betrayed. And I was very much sincere with him to the point that I defended him to my family and friends who disliked him. Apparently, jail time didn't reform him at all because he did again what got him into trouble in the first place. And it doesn't matter if he's no longer chatting with women from Arizona or that he introduced me to his friends and siblings over the phone. Those acts do not erase the fact that he just used me and played with my emotions and vulnerabilities.

Out of anger for learning about his online infidelity the second time, I called him. My phone credits were limited, so he called back and we talked for two hours. He denied registering another account and flirting with other women online. I told him that I'm mad, yet at the same time I pity him because he's really sick—a pathological liar and porn addict. I told him to stop victimizing women, for he has two daughters whom he would not want to be hurt the way I got hurt by him. Knowing what I know now about sociopathy, it's doubtful if being sent back to jail and attending classes to modify his thought process and behavior could transform him.

I know by this time some of you are thinking how stupid and ridiculous I am for even spending time to narrate this whole drama. It was an online LDR thing, yes...but somehow, the way we behave online speaks of how we behave offline as well. And I was very much sincere with him, believing that we had a commitment.

I'm sure most of you will tell me to move on and celebrate because I got out of a relationship with a man who is troubled. And I agree with you. But at this time, I'm struggling to do that. And if you ask me why I fell for someone like him...I've got no answer to give because it's hard to rationalize something irrational.

What G did to me is really painful. I could have offered the love I gave him to someone deserving. I really thought my search for my second and last mate is finally over with him, but I was wrong. And from this hurt, I find myself becoming ambivalent—shaking my way towards reaching the healing point because I'm still blaming myself for what happened, for allowing a man like him into my life simply because I succumbed to the loneliness of being a single mom, failing to love myself positively. I long to love and be loved, but not the way he subjected me to. It's unfair, but I know I need to forgive myself—and also forgive him before I could move on completely.

Dreams come true

Juanita's story illustrates an important reason why we fall for sociopaths: They promise to make our dreams come true, and we believe them.

This is especially true with online dating. As explained on Lovefraud's *Online Seduction* page, when we correspond with someone over the Internet, vital information is missing. We can't evaluate the person's appearance, body language, grooming and tone of voice. We don't even know for sure if we're corresponding with a man or a woman.

With so much information missing, what do we do? We imagine the person to be what we want him or her to be.

And, according to Dr. Esther Gwinnell, author of a book called *Online Seductions*, we take it a step further. "Because you have none of the usual cues to bring you back to reality," she writes, "you may begin to attribute important qualities to the person, especially idealistic and romantic qualities."

Trapped and lonely, Juanita was dreaming of love, and thought she'd found what she was looking for. The American, however, simply played with her dreams, perhaps just to amuse himself.

That's why this whole experience was so painful for Juanita. Even though she talked to the American frequently, she was never physically with him. Much of the relationship, therefore, was in her own mind. She couldn't end the relationship by kicking the guy out the door. She had to kick him out of her mind — and out of her dreams.

9 questions to help you discern if your caring, helpful partner is faking it

She makes you drinks and home-cooked meals. He cuts your lawn and fixes your car. Your new romantic interest just can't seem to do enough for you. You never felt so cared for. It must be love!

Maybe it is. Or maybe it's a sociopath who is trying to soften you up for later exploitation.

I've often written on Lovefraud that sociopaths do not have the ability to be caregivers. Many readers find this confusing — the sociopath they know was always doing things for them. So let me explain. First, some background.

Three components of romantic love

The core of sociopathic personality disorders is an inability to love. What, exactly does this mean?

Scientists have determined that romantic love has three components. They are:

- Attachment — people who are in love want to be with their special person
- Sex — for physical closeness and procreation
- Caregiving — people who are in love want to take care of their special person. They are truly concerned about their partner's wellbeing and growth, and want the best for their partner.

Real love includes all three parts. Sociopaths can do the first two components — they want to be with the object of their desire, and they certainly want sex. But when it comes to caregiving, they simply cannot put the needs of someone else before their own.

Sociopaths are not truly interested in their partner's health, growth or wellbeing. They are only interested in what their partner can do for them, or in how their partner's achievements reflect on them.

It's not caring; it's seduction

Sociopaths frequently engage in caring behavior — professionals call it "pro-social behavior" — in the beginning of the involvement, when they are trying to reel you in. In fact, doing things for you is a function of love bombing. It's one of the ways that they shower you with attention and affection.

This apparent caregiving also speeds the relationship up. Why? It makes you feel that you need to reciprocate. So you start doing things for them. Your emotional investment grows, pulling you deeper into the relationship.

You're being seduced, but you might not see their true agenda right away. Some sociopaths are in for the long con. They may have targeted your assets, and if it takes them five to 10 years to get your money, they'll continue playing the game. Or, they may be using their involvement with you as cover for a secret double life.

Here's what you need to know: When sociopaths care for you, they always have an ulterior motive.

Real caring or a sociopath?

Of course, when someone really does love you, he or she will do things for you. So how do you know if you've met your true love, or a sociopath? The following nine questions will help you discern the truth.

1. How does your partner treat other people, especially wait staff in restaurants and clerks in stores? Is he or she rude, demanding and critical — totally different from how you are treated?
2. Does your partner's actions match his or her words? If your partner promises to do something or be somewhere, does he or she follow through?

3. When your partner does nice things for you, is it help that you really want or need, or is the partner doing things that he or she likes to do? What happens when you ask your partner to do something that he or she doesn't like, or would be an inconvenience?
4. What happens when you're sick? This one is tricky, and can vary depending on where you are in the seduction process. If the sociopath is still reeling you in, he or she can dote on you, bring you everything you need, and never leaver your side. But when sociopaths perceive that you are hooked, typically they won't lift a finger to help you.
5. Sociopathy isn't one trait or behavior, it's a collection of traits and behaviors. So do you see other warning signs of sociopathy? If you don't know what to look for, they are thoroughly explained in my book, *Red Flags of Love Fraud – 10 signs you're dating a sociopath*.
6. If your partner has children, how does he or she treat them? Look closely. Is the parent truly concerned about the children's welfare? Or is the parent more interested in how the kids make him or her look?
7. Is your partner really helping you — or is he or she exerting control over you? For example, some sociopaths start driving their partners around. They act like they're helping, but what they are really doing is controlling their partners' movements.
8. Does your partner's caring behavior ramp up when you start pulling away? That means he or she is turning on the love bombing again.
9. Did you in the beginning, or at any point in your involvement, have a bad feeling about your partner? Did you sense that something wasn't right? Your instincts are designed to warn you about predators. Trust your instincts.

10 reasons why the fireworks of a romance with a sociopath are duds

In honor of July 4th, let's talk about fireworks — the really dangerous kind. These are the fireworks that you feel exploding all around you early in your relationship with someone who later turns out to be a sociopath. Here's what you see and experience, and what it really going on.

1. You see: Nonstop texts, emails and social media postings

Reality: You're not the only one receiving them. The Internet and social media make it easy for sociopaths to work multiple targets at once, and they do.

2. You experience: Conversations that last for hours

Reality: The sociopath is pumping you for information, which he/she will later use to manipulate you.

3. You experience: Nonstop dates, get-togethers — the sociopath always wants to be with you

Reality: The sociopath knows you're hooked, and he/she is reeling you in.

4. You receive: Cute little gifts, or even expensive gifts

Reality: There's a good chance they're either recycled or stolen from another partner.

5. You experience: Wild, passionate, "rock your world" sex

Reality: Sociopaths (both male and female) have excess testosterone, engage frequently and get bored easily. You are, and always will be, one of many partners.

6. You hear: "I love you," and your heart soars

Reality: It's a lie, because sociopaths cannot love. But they know if they say, "I love you," they get what they want.

7. You see: Moist eyes, or even tears rolling down the cheek

Reality: Crying by sociopaths isn't a sign of pain or sadness. It's an act designed to make you feel sorry for them — and give them what they want.

8. You get: Multiple phone calls a day, just to say "hello"

Reality: The sociopath is checking up on you, and slowly establishing control over you.

9. You hear: "We're soul mates!" and you feel like you've found the one you've been waiting for all your life.

Reality: This isn't a deep truth springing forth from the sociopath. It's a tactic that he/she knows works, because it's been used before.

10. You hear: Promises of "happily ever after"

Reality: Sociopaths set their hooks deep within you by promising to make your dreams come true. In the end, it's entrapment.

Letter to Lovefraud:
He flat out admits he is a sociopath

Editor's note: The following letter was sent by 26-year-old Lovefraud reader, "Clarissa." Names have been changed.

My name is Clarissa. I have just ended a relationship with someone who I believe is a sociopath. I'm having a difficult time accepting and trying to understand this relationship and getting over the events that occurred.

Reconnecting with Blain after so many years

I will call my ex "Blain." I had dated him briefly in high school and broke up with him. He randomly contacted me online 9 years later and was very persistent in me going for a coffee with him. At first I ignored him but when I saw he kept messaging me I said ok, I ended up meeting him and didn't think anything of him except I found him a little creepy (something about his stare).

At this time I worked late and had to take the subway late at night. He would always offer to pick me up from work and I found that nice and flattering (as he was making such an effort to see me even though my schedule was so difficult). I kept spending time with him almost every day. I began to enjoy his company and shared a lot of personal information with him. He seemed so perfect, listening to me and always being there. He had told me that once he "caught feelings for someone" he would usually disconnect from the relationship.

Things continued this way before I noticed we were seeing

each other every day and he was always in contact with me, texting me, calling me, always asking what I was doing. He would ask me a lot of questions about myself, yet he wasn't very open or wouldn't really elaborate about himself (like what he did for work).

Blain becomes a different person

Within the first couple of months he was very attentive and would take me out for dinners. I began to develop an emotional attachment to him. However, I began to notice he would randomly send me strange texts and started criticizing certain things about me; he would call me an alcoholic if I wanted to go for a drink when it wasn't his idea. He started slowly telling me who was right for me out of my friends and who wasn't. Even so much as telling me my friends did not want anything good for me.

He had bought me an expensive phone after we dated for about 3 months. One day I noticed he hadn't called me all day, which never happened. I finally called him in the evening and he was very rude and told me he did not want to be with me anymore. I was extremely upset and pleaded him to tell me why, he was reluctant to answer. He finally told me he doesn't want a girl like me because I liked one of my classmate's (male) photos on Facebook. We ended up getting into a huge fight over it and I begged him to come and see me. After this incident he started becoming a different person.

Obsessed with checking my phone

He became obsessed with checking my phone (the one he had bought me). He would get mad at me for the smallest reasons such as me interrupting him while he was speaking, making plans with my friends, drinking if I wasn't with him or even when I was with him.

At this point I found myself walking on eggshells always trying to avoid him getting mad at me, which would lead to what I called the "punishment" of him being cold and rude to me. I was afraid to make plans with my friends. He never told me not to, he would rather tell me "go make plans" in a spiteful way, like you will see what happens if and when you do.

When I did go see my friends I would be scared to tell him so I would tell him I was doing other things. He would interrogate to the point I was extremely uncomfortable and tell him the truth. When I would tell him the truth he would consistently accuse me of being a liar over and over, and almost used it as an excuse to question my every move. If there was something I didn't tell him he would call me a liar and would say he hates liars. He never wanted to trust me — almost as if it was more convenient this way for him.

Moody, Distrustful and Fired

All this behavior started to multiply. He became extremely moody and started checking my phone on a regular basis — to the point where if my phone wasn't on the dashboard in the car he would accuse me of hiding something. Not to mention he had two phones and one was used for "business." I had never looked at his phones.

I started to catch on and told him he was very jealous and paranoid, he denied this and told me he was acting this way because I lied to him in the past. I told him that he is so controlling and his behavior makes me uncomfortable and how does he expect me to be open about everything when he gets mad at me over everything and criticizes my every move.

He didn't like my job, which had me dealing with people in a high-end hotel. He would constantly ask me, did you ever go home with anyone you met there or had any relations, which I never did. He told me that job was bad for me. Eventually I got fired from this job, which left me in a very bad place.

At this point he pretty much isolated me from all of my friends, so all I had left was him. I started feeling terrible anxiety. One of my long time friends contacted me, and Blain told me he thought it was embarrassing if I was friends with him and wouldn't be with me if I was friends with this person.

One time when he saw I spoke to this friend, and when Blain asked me I denied it. He forced me to check my phone and when he saw the phone call he threw a huge fit, swearing and yelling at me in a public place (pharmacy). He again threatened to break up with me and when I tried to calm him down he literally pushed me so hard away from him.

We had nothing

The controlling got worse until I was clearly unhappy, since I wasn't working. It appeared he had a lot of free time on his hands. He would always want to spend time with me every day, until the point came were we had nothing to talk about anymore.

He told me he was working and he had all these big plans, and he was working on something new. He later admitted to me he was never working during this time. When I wanted to go out like we did in the beginning of the relationship, he would tell me he has no money and that I was too used to how things were in the beginning, that I wasn't happy unless he spent money on me (which was never the case).

Old friends and new friends don't mix

One day I decided to go for lunch with a childhood friend. He had known I have been friends with him forever. I was scared to tell Blain this and told him I had gone with my mom. While I was having lunch, he had driven by my house to see which car I was in and was texting me "where are you — I know where you are."

I told him the truth and he broke up with me stating that I'm a liar and he doesn't want a girl that goes for lunch with another guy and lies (even though he had known he was a good friend of my mine since we were kids.) HE SAID YOU EITHER DROP YOUR FRIEND OR INTRODUCE ME TO HIM (my friend hated him since high school because he said his stare made him uncomfortable).

I'm a sociopath, you're a liar

Blain told me he just can't live with that at all. When he was breaking up with me he stated he was a sociopath and had roaches in his head. When I asked him to elaborate he would tell me he will go to any lengths to get what he wants and that he's done a lot of things in his life he is not proud of.

Within hours of breaking up with me he was contacting me non-stop. I felt guilty because Blain's birthday was a day before he broke up with me. I begged him and pleaded him to forgive me until he did, but not fully. He would consistently call me a liar again.

Eventually I told him we couldn't be together and he did everything in his power to get me back. My parents and friends started hating him because they long noticed his negative effect on me. I was very hesitant to take him back at this point and he had promised he would never hurt me again and would never leave me, that he loved me. Then he stated that he only realized he loved me when he broke up with me, which did not make sense, since he had told me he loved me previously. I had the worst feeling about taking him back and eventually since he was so persistent I did.

Not good enough to meet the parents

For about a month, he was on his best behavior. After a month I started to see his old self slowly re-appear. He would have sudden mood swings to the point where I didn't even know what mood he would wake up in and how he would treat me that day. He started complaining about how little sex we were having in comparison to the beginning of the relationship (which was all the time because I almost felt obligated to. If I didn't he would get mad at me or act unsatisfied).

We both lived with our parents and he never made any effort to introduce me to his parents and therefore he would never invite me over when his parents were home. When I brought this up to him he made excuses like I didn't hold the fork in the right hand when I ate and later said he was joking.

I had told him I didn't want to have sex in his car any more, that it degraded me and made me uncomfortable. He did not like this and threw a tantrum and even tried to manipulate me into feeling guilty, like I wasn't pleasing him as a man. He once even told me that if I didn't please him he would find someone who would.

At this point I was confused and told him he was a manipulator and his behavior was disgusting and immature. He admitted to his behavior and said he can't believe himself and how's he's acting, but a day later would go back to complaining and draining my energy over this issue.

During this time I started noticing I was losing my attraction to him, that his immaturity had completely turned me off. I would notice he would sit there and expect me to make a move on him, and when I didn't, he would treat me badly (ie."punish me"). I started questioning if I even enjoy his company, because of his constant interrogations, accusations and criticism (which he stated he wanted to better me).

There was so much inconsistency with what he said, based on his moods. After he could tell me he was crazy, within 20 minutes he would act like he never said and anything and called me crazy. He even told me he had an out of body experience, where he looked in the mirror and didn't recognize himself, that he often looks in the mirror and feels incredibly angry.

It's over

I had called an old friend one day just to say hi. After the phone rang twice, I had hung up before he answered and later that evening I met up with Blain. As soon as Blain saw my phone light up he got angry and said, "You have a message, why is your phone on silent. What are you hiding from me?"

I got scared and told him it was my friend calling from his work number. He wanted me to call that person back in front of him and I wouldn't. He called me the next day and said I will either tell him the truth or we are done.

That same day I met Blain after work. I had to use the washroom so he stopped by an ice cream shop. I asked Blain to join me and/or if he wanted anything.

While I went to use the bathroom he had completely checked my phone and was standing outside the ice cream shop with a very scary intense stare. I had asked if he wanted any of my ice cream and he replied no, I checked your phone lets read it together. I refused. It humiliated me. I had told him it wasn't like what he thought nothing happened. He didn't want to hear it.

Letter to Lovefraud: He flat out admits he is a sociopath

This was also 2 weeks before my birthday. He dropped me off at home and told me he needs space. I had not spoken to him in 10 days — he didn't call and I didn't either.

After 10 days he began calling and texting me non-stop I ignored him for 3 days and he didn't stop. Eventually I answered and told him I want nothing to do with him any longer. That didn't stop him. He mailed flowers to my work, bought me a very expensive birthday gift, and flowers again and I still refused to get back with him.

He still continues to contact me randomly either asking to talk, telling me he loves me, at times he admits he's wrong and at times he gets angry and says hurtful things. He consistently asks me over and over if I'm seeing someone else. I tell him after such an unhealthy relationship it's very hard to get into another relationship. He constantly asks if I'm sleeping with someone and I tell him honestly that I have not. I even told him that it seems to me that he was always so paranoid of me cheating is because he was doing it himself; since I never did, nor did I question him about it. He says he never did, that he's not a traitor, but I tell him he would never admit to it regardless.

As of today he just says, "I made a mistake. I may be wrong at times — don't be angry at me. I never wanted anything bad for you." I was going to put a ring on it. It truly seems he just doesn't feel any empathy or doesn't realize how his actions affect others, and just says things without really meaning it.

Based on your previous experience I know you have a good understanding of sociopaths' behavior. Does Blain fit the characteristics? This relationship really took a toll on my emotional well-being. Please give me some advice based on your opinion?

Clarissa

Donna Andersen responds

Yes, Blain is a sociopath. In fact, he is a textbook case, which is why I wanted to post your letter. If any Lovefraud reader sees this type of behavior, know that you're dealing with a sociopath. It will never get better. You should end the relationship.

Emotional and psychological abuse, described by 12 Lovefraud readers

What does emotional and psychological abuse look like? Here are a dozen examples provided by respondents to the Lovefraud Senior Sociopath Survey:

1. Any arguments that happened as a result of me bringing up something he had done or said were always flipped to be my fault and I would end up crying and apologising and he would withhold affection.
2. He would tell me that I was perfect and then if he didn't like my behavior he would say I needed to change
3. Twist words, made me feel that it was my fault, would be over the top flattering then create a false sense of trust then use information to put me down. Would make me feel anxious, never knowing when he'd turn up, would ask me to do things, but if I refused, was made to feel stupid. Emotional distressing.
4. Control food in the house, what I would be allowed to eat. Made me go to the gym with him every day. I got too thin but he liked me that way. He made all the terms in the relationship. Would triangulate me with old girlfriends and young pretty girls telling me I'm jealous and insecure.

Emotional and psychological abuse, described by 12 Lovefraud readers

5. Immediately after asking a question, he would bombard me with more and take the conversation in a different direction. Then he would point out my "flaws" and say we needed to "work on" my "development and growth." He avoided answering questions by humiliating me for asking them.
6. Did not like to go out or travel, I was not allowed to do anything without his permission. He would dismiss all my opinions and treat me like I was self centered and selfish. Especially if I tried to stand up to him.
7. Verbally abusive, temper tantrums. Silent treatment when he did not get his way. Cursed and yelled a lot.
8. He would never answer a question. He would keep information from me about his schedule/trips. He would tell his son to ignore me. He would lie. He would take my things and when I asked him if he had seen them he said no. Then my things would be back in their place and he'd tell me I was crazy and suffered from mental health problems.
9. Silent treatment, pouting, verbal abuse
10. Made me feel that if I didn't look, behave, act like he wanted, others would think less of me. He was a loner, only wanted to be with me. I thought it was because I was special to him. It was because he was distancing me from everyone else — removing my support.
11. Always had an answer for everything. It was never his fault; he would always manage to twist everything. Would make you feel you are the guilty one even when you aren't.
12. Intermittent reinforcement, gaslighting, stonewalling, smear campaign, goading, lies upon lies, belittling, humiliating, ghosting (not answering texts, emails, calls), missing important appointments, the list goes on....

Examples like these will be part of my upcoming book, *Senior Sociopaths — How to Recognize and Escape Lifelong Abusers*. More than 2,000 Lovefraud readers completed the initial senior sociopath survey, providing a wealth of information about their experiences with sociopaths over the age of 50.

A total of 512 respondents described romantic relationships with people who were already over 50 when they met and turned out to be disordered. Ninety-one percent of the respondents said they endured emotional abuse, and 84% were psychologically abused.

Letter to Lovefraud: Should I warn the next victim?

Lovefraud received the following email from a reader who posts as "forever_me:"

Hello. I am looking for some guidance. I was in a romantic relationship with a P for over 2 years, but just broke it off earlier this week. I discovered that he was using an online dating site and was able to access it because I knew the patterns of his passwords. I created a bogus profile on the same website and contacted one of the women he was messaging. She was shocked to hear from me because my P told her he was single and not dating anyone. What was worse was that they had engaged in unprotected sex a few days before my P and I had unprotected sex. We agreed to meet each other to discuss the details of our relationships with this man. She had been dating him for just over a month.

After my conversation with this woman, I wanted answers from my P, although at this time I didn't realize that was what he was. I was persistent in my confrontation with him, which took 3 hours of dealing with blatant lie after lie. He initially denied dating anyone else or knowing about the dating site, then claimed he was letting a friend use his identity to cheat on a fiance, then finally admitted he did go on a few dates with the woman I had contacted through the site. However, he swore that he'd never had sex with her or anyone else since we'd been together. In fact, the woman I met was actually stalking him and trying to turn me against him since he rejected her. I eventually walked out the door when he told me he was sorry, not for his actions, but because I was under the misunderstanding we were a couple instead of just friends with benefits. It is worth noting that during the course of our dialogue, he casually picked up the newspaper to read it and briefly watched the local news as if we were just having a typical evening together.

I was so bewildered by his lies and behavior after I left that I began searching the internet and stumbled upon this blog. Reading the many entries made me realize that I had been involved with a P. All the little red flags added up and I'm coming to terms with the truth. This site has expedited my healing and I thank everyone involved for that!

Now my conscience is wondering if I should continue to warn other women about him? He changed his password but I have once again figured it out. The woman I contacted before was glad I did. I don't plan to meet any of these women going forward, but just send them a note of concern under cover to let them know what to watch for if they decide to date him. I know I can't do this forever since he could change his password again or switch dating sites, and I need to move on with my life as well. The advice I've read here says I should just walk away since I have no financial, legal, or career ties to him. Several women are currently corresponding with him. Since he's independently wealthy, handsome, and charming, they'll be hooked soon enough. Should I just let it go or contact these women knowing I'll save a few of them from the pain he'll surely inflict?

Should she try to warn the next victim, or shouldn't she? This has been the topic of much debate here on Lovefraud. I last wrote about this topic in a blog post back in 2007. But it's an important issue, so let's discuss it again.

If you're considering warning others about the sociopath, here are factors to consider:

1. Can you warn someone safely?

The first thing to consider, of course, is your physical safety. If the sociopath you were involved with has a history of violence, even if the violence was never directed towards you, I would urge caution.

But safety involves more than worries about violence. Consider also your legal and financial status. If you are in the midst of a divorce or custody battle with your ex, you do not want to do anything that will jeopardize your case, your job, or anything else that he may be able to damage through accusations.

No matter how badly you may feel for the next target, you must put yourself first.

2. What is your emotional state?

Relationships with sociopaths inflict emotional and psychological damage on us. The best way to recover from the damage is to have No Contact with the sociopath.

Tracking a sociopath's actions is sometimes gratifying, however, because we feel like we're no longer being conned. We see through the mask. We know what he or she is up to. In a way, it's a boost to our trampled self-esteem to be on to the con. And yes, we probably have to admit to wanting a taste of revenge by ruining the sociopath's game.

But even if we're not talking to the sociopath, or sending email, we have to remember that keeping tabs, and warning others, is a form of contact. As we say here on Lovefraud, the predator is still renting space in our brains.

So, before you do it, think about where you are in your recovery. Can you do this and continue to heal?

3. Will the victim's reaction affect you?

We know how good the sociopaths are, because we were hooked. Think of how the sociopath described his or her prior involvements to you. Did he say his ex-wives were mentally disturbed? Did she say her ex-husband was a stalker? Well, that's what is now being said about you.

The sociopath is already running a smear campaign to discredit anything that you may say. At the same time, the sociopath is love bombing the new victim. He or she is primed to disbelieve you.

If the new victim blows you off, can you just walk away?

My view

In my personal opinion, if you can warn the next victim without jeopardizing your own safety and recovery, I think you should at least try.

I've heard of cases where the victim was grateful for the warning and got out. I've heard of cases where the next victim has refused to listen and stayed with the sociopath. And I've heard of cases where the victim stayed for a while, then started to see the bad behavior, remembered the warning, and got out.

I know that since I've posted the information online about my ex-husband, James Montgomery, at least seven women have contacted me to thank me for the warning. They Googled his name, found Lovefraud, and dumped him. I don't know how many may have dumped him without telling me. This makes me feel good.

However, James Montgomery is on the other side of the world. I've had a chance to recover and move on. He can't damage me.

So if you feel like you need to warn others, remember this: Your first obligation is to yourself. Do what you must do for your own recovery. If you can assist others without hurting yourself, that is icing on the cake.

Here's the absolutely best way to protect yourself from sociopaths

Yes, you can avoid letting a sociopath into your life. All you have to do is listen to your intuition.

Security expert Gavin deBecker, who wrote *The Gift of Fear*, explains that intuition evolved within us over the millennia for one reason: To protect us from predators. Sociopaths are predators, and our intuition will warn us about them.

The key is to pay attention.

Sometimes the warning is blatant — one woman told me about feeling instantly terrified when a man approached her. But instead of heeding her internal warning, she berated herself for being judgmental — after all, the man had done nothing to her. She talked to him; they became romantically involved; he was, in fact, a sociopath; it ended in disaster.

She certainly isn't the only person with this experience. I specifically asked about intuition in the 2011 Lovefraud Romantic Partner Survey, which drew 1,352 responses. The question was, "In the beginning of the of the involvement, did you have a gut feeling or intuition that something wasn't right about the person or the relationship?" A whopping 71 percent of respondents answered yes. Forty percent ignored their intuition and continued the relationship anyway — much to their later regret.

You're probably not accustomed to making a decision about someone based simply on your gut feelings. After all, deBecker says, "Intuition is usually looked upon by us thoughtful Western beings with contempt." We're indoctrinated with the idea that decisions should be based on logic, rational deliberation and evidence, not feelings.

Plus, we usually want to believe the sociopath. He or she is telling us exactly what we want to hear. So we override our deep internal knowing and walk into the trap.

Intuitive warnings about someone may appear as:

- Sudden fear
- An instant dislike
- A vague sense of unease
- Feeling creeped out
- Hair standing up on the back of your neck
- A sense that something isn't right
- You react to a specific behavior with, "Huh? What was that?"

If you search the Internet, you'll surely find plenty of checklists that indicate sociopathic behavior. I developed one for Lovefraud called, Is your partner a sociopath?

Checklists of sociopathic traits are certainly helpful for validation. But what makes you go looking for checklists in the first place? Your sense that something is off — in other words, your intuition.

Your intuition, instinct, gut feeling — whatever you want to call it — is a built-in early warning system. By committing to take action based on what your internal warning system tells you, you will save yourself a lot of heartache.

How knowing the truth about sociopaths changes everything

Lovefraud received the following email from a reader whom we'll call "Louisa."

I was in a relationship with someone that constantly cheated, and cried and begged me back. Five years of thinking we were "working through problems," sharing every detail about myself, supporting him and bailing him out of his obligations while struggling with my own.

It all ended a couple of weeks ago when I found out he was molesting my 10 year old daughter and her friend...

I'm feeling devastated. Reading all I have and looking back I'm resentful to myself for staying and thinking it was my best friend and soul mate. I paid a price beyond what I ever thought I could have.

He is in jail and took a plea bargain for the charges. Which he admitted to for some agenda.

He tried to call me collect from jail, to which I obtained a restraining order for myself (my child received one immediately).

How did I let it come to this? Why do I hurt so immensely yet feel stronger than I ever have? How do I help my daughter and work through my guilt?

Donna Andersen responds

Louisa,
First of all, I am so sorry for what you, your daughter and your

daughter's friend have experienced. It is devastating. I am glad the perp is in jail, and will have a record as a sex offender for the rest of his life.

You asked several questions at the end of your email. You are in pain, and rightfully so. But the answer to all of your questions is the same: Previously, you did not know the truth, and now you do.

The key strategy sociopaths use to infiltrate our lives and exploit us is deception. The problem with deception, of course, is that we don't know it is happening.

You may be berating yourself, feeling like you "should have known." How? You don't know what you don't know.

Sociopaths are expert liars. Human beings, however, are lousy lie detectors. Research has shown that people can spot liars only 53% of the time. That's about as good as flipping a coin.

So to address your questions:

How did you let it come to this?

You didn't know the truth — that he is a sociopath. And you probably didn't know the larger truth, either — that sociopaths, human predators, live among us.

Why do you hurt immensely yet feel stronger than ever?

Because now you know the truth. Now you know that he was lying from the very beginning of your involvement. Now you know that he was exploiting you. Learning the truth enabled you to take decisive action — and he is in jail.

How do you help your daughter?

By teaching her the truth — evil exists. Sociopaths exist. But sometimes these evil sociopaths pretend to be good and loving. We need to be on the lookout for them.

Finally, how do you work through your guilt?

By recognizing that you have now learned an important truth that you did not know before: Human beings are hardwired to trust and love — except for sociopaths. These people are capable

How knowing the truth about sociopaths changes everything

of professing their love, but when they do, they are lying, because they are incapable of truly feeling love.

Sometimes we learn the truth the hard way, as you did. But once we know it, we can't unlearn it. So even though the discovery was extremely painful, knowing the truth can serve to protect you and the girls for the rest of your lives.

About the author

Donna Andersen is author of Lovefraud.com, a website that teaches people to recognize and recover from sociopaths. She is also author of *Red Flags of Love Fraud—10 signs you're dating a sociopath* and the *Red Flags of Love Fraud Workbook*.

Donna learned about sociopaths the hard way—by marrying one. She tells the whole outrageous story in her first book, *Love Fraud—How marriage to a sociopath fulfilled my spiritual plan*. The book was awarded five stars by the Midwest Book Review.

Donna founded Lovefraud Education and Recovery. The nonprofit offers online webinars to help professionals and the public spot, escape and recover from narcissists, antisocials, psychopaths and other manipulators. She is co-author of a scientific paper about therapy for victims of sociopaths, and has presented research to the Society for the Scientific Study of Psychopathy.

Donna has appeared on television shows including *Insight* in Australia, *ABC News 20/20*, *Who the Bleep Did I Marry?*, *My Life is a Lifetime Movie*, *Handsome Devils* and *The Ricki Lake Show*. She has been interviewed for multiple radio shows, print articles and web posts.

Donna graduated summa cum laude from the Syracuse University with degrees in magazine journalism and psychology. She was the original editor of Atlantic City Magazine, and then founded a boutique advertising agency, Donna Andersen Copywriting, in 1983. Her portfolio includes multimedia scriptwriting, freelance magazine articles, newsletters, web content and more.

Donna is happily remarried, proving that recovery from betrayal is possible.

Lightning Source UK Ltd.
Milton Keynes UK
UKHW021329190320
360610UK00008B/1265